GOOD LESSONS FROM BAD GUYS

Mike O'Neal

ISBN: 978-0-89098-892-3

©2018 by 21st Century Christian

2809 12th Ave S, Nashville, TN 37204

All rights reserved.

Cover design by Jonathan Edelhuber

Preface and Acknowledgements

I n the not-too-distant past, I taught a Bible school class on the topic of David. A sweet Christian woman, whom I had known for years, regularly attended each week. In fact, she attended most activities anytime the church's doors were open. Through the years, she had probably listened to around 5,000 sermons and participated in another 6,000 Bible classes and devotionals. She also taught in our children's education program and during Vacation Bible School. This lady was thoroughly acquainted with the Bible and its stories. After teaching a class on David's encounter with Nabal, she quietly pulled me aside, and started shaking her head as she said, "Over all these years I do not recall hearing a sermon or lesson on this story." Somewhat surprised to hear her make such a remark, I admitted to its lesser-known status, while storing away her comment.

As I continued to study God's Word, I started to notice a number of fairly short stories, which often seemed rather obscure. Most of them involved one or more unsavory characters. Many times, these stories served as an excursion from the main narrative. I remember asking myself, *Why are these stories here? Are there important lessons that God wants us to learn from them?* These reflective inquiries served as the genesis for this book and imparted a passion within me to reveal the lessons contained in these stories.

Some of these stories may be new to you; some may not be. But no matter what the case, I believe you will be exposed to some fresh material that you can use in our contemporary settings. All of the stories involve some of the Bible's bad actors, and most are a little obscure, though not all of them. God has placed them in His Word for a reason, so let's try to understand what He would like us to glean from them.

To my good friend, Gayle Griffin, I truly appreciate the many hours you spent in editing *Good Lessons from Bad Guys*. My writing style has some rough edges, and your skillful and thoughtful review helped make this book a more appealing read. Your ministry in this regard, not only aided myself, but serves others as they hopefully draw closer to God through the pages of this book. I know the time and energy that you expended took you away from your loved ones and personal interests, and I am forever grateful for your sacrifices in this regard.

I want to thank Professor Allen Black, Dean at the Harding School of Theology, for helping clarify a particular passage in Acts for me. I also want to continue to thank my many professors and the librarians at this august graduate school. You prepared me to take on such writing tasks and have thus contributed to this book in many indirect ways.

I am also grateful to my minister friends, Mike Shumate and Bob Bliss, who allowed me to share some of the approaches I was taking in the book. Thank you for providing a listening ear and thoughtful remarks. Also, the resources you provided to me were instrumental in putting a couple of the chapters together.

It's nice when people place their confidence in you, and that's what my publisher, 21st Century Christian, has done in my regard. Thank you so much for allowing me to serve God in a writing capacity. Your company has personally blessed me in many ways, and I am truly grateful that you put your faith in me to put this project together.

To my wife, thank you for walking by my side during this journey and especially for allowing me to read aloud sections of the manuscript to you. Your patient listening made a positive impact on the books readability, and I know this often occurred when you were tired from a busy day. Also, thank you for reading the text along the way as well as discussing some of the concepts and stories I was considering to use in the book.

Lastly, to the readers, I thank you for considering to read this book. As a writer, I find it an honor, as well as humbling, for others to spend their valuable time exploring the pages of my books. I can guarantee you that this book was a work of passion, prayed over, and well researched. I truly believe you will be spiritually enriched by the book's contents. I pray that God will draw you closer to Him as you delve into this book and may it serve as a tool to help form you in the image of His Son.

To my loving God, I praise Your holy name and offer thanksgiving and all the glory to You.

Table of Contents

CHAPTER 1

Nabal

Provoked by a Fool

Do not answer a fool according to his folly,
Or you will also be like him.

(Proverbs 26:4)

Human space flight is inherently a dangerous business. A launch vehicle's high-energy systems present many hazardous concerns because of their explosive and often toxic nature. During launch and ascent, the vehicle must operate safely under some extreme conditions if it is to deliver its precious cargo intact. One of the more complicated issues facing early rocket designers (who used liquid rocket engines) was a phenomenon referred to as pogo. Pogo is a thrust-axis vibration of the vehicle that can occur due to surges in thrust and propellant feedline pressures. For the crew, severe oscillations may result in crippling pain, which could impair their ability to perform required tasks. For the vehicle, damage may occur to its systems if the vibrations become too violent and then possibly even trigger a catastrophic event. By the way, the space lingo term *pogo* comes from the similar linear bouncing effect you get from a pogo stick.[1]

To address the pogo effect, you basically need a shock absorber to dampen out the oscillations in the propellant lines. The designers of the Space Shuttle Main Engines dealt with this troublesome problem by installing an accumulator in the liquid oxygen feedlines that contains baffles and is charged with gaseous oxygen to diminish any pressure surges thus preventing the pogo vibrations.

By now you may be asking, *Why in the world has he introduced this nerdy technical information?* Actually, it's for a good reason. We all tend to need a pogo suppression system at times. I am sure you can remember a circumstance in your life when your emotions and actions escalated an already unpleasant situation. When someone says or does something hurtful to us, an unhealthy "vibration" internally starts. And if left unchecked, what comes next usually isn't pretty. In such times, we need a "pogo suppressor" to come alongside us before we lash out and inflict unnecessary pain, resulting in irreparable damage to a valued relationship. Someone who knows us can calm us, and reason with us before the fireworks start. Even the "sweet psalmist of Israel" needed a "pogo suppressor" to enter his life and cool his surging fury on one occasion.

When Goodness Turns to Rage

When David was fleeing for his life from crazed King Saul, he took those in his charge to a wilderness at the southern border of Judah. To create good will with his new neighbors and future subjects, David's men voluntarily guarded over a local rich man's flocks of sheep and goats. Such a service should have been held in high regard due to the potential presence of marauding bands of thieves and Judah's enemies, but the story turns ugly when David seeks a charitable reward for their services. As we turn to 1 Samuel 25, let's explore the three main players in this story, as several important lessons wait for us there.

The Fool

Have you ever introduced someone by their possessions before giving their name? It isn't likely, unless you want that individual to be identified by their material assets and wealth. Yet, that was how the narrator chose to introduce Nabal to his readers. His possessions and wealth defined him, and that fact sheds a revealing light on his character.

We learn of his name only after the author interrupted the flow of the story to provide us with a side remark that also describes his demeanor. Nabal was not only "filthy" rich, he was "harsh and evil in his dealings" (v. 3). In other words, he treated others cruelly and dealt dishonestly with those whom he conducted business, taking advantage of them for his personal gain.

Nabal means "fool." Obviously, no one's parents would give their child such a name, so it was probably a nickname used behind his back by those he had victimized by his foolhardy behavior. But don't be misled, Nabal was no simpleton or unintelligent. His reasoning and resultant conduct came from a perverted set of values. Solomon and David aptly described a "fool's" character and twisted ways in the following proverbs and psalm, providing us with some insight on what to expect out of Nabal the fool.

> The fear of the LORD is the beginning of knowledge; Fools despise wisdom and instruction (Proverbs 1:7).
>
> Doing wickedness is like sport to a fool, and *so is* wisdom to a man of understanding (Proverbs 10:23).
>
> The way of a fool is right in his own eyes, but a wise man is he who listens to counsel (Proverbs 12:15).
>
> Desire realized is sweet to the soul, but it is an abomination to fools to turn away from evil (Proverbs 13:19).
>
> The wisdom of the sensible is to understand his way, but the foolishness of fools is deceit (Proverbs 14:8).
>
> A wise man is cautious and turns away from evil, But a fool is arrogant and careless (Proverbs 14:16).
>
> A fool does not delight in understanding, but only in revealing his own mind (Proverbs 18:2).

The fool has said in his heart, "There is no God"...(Psalms 14:1).

The above fairly well depicts the attitudes and practices exhibited by Nabal in our story. As you shall see, his self-righteousness, self-centeredness, and materialistic nature guided his way in life. He had no regard for God's wisdom. Nabal's god was Nabal. He had no room for God's ways because it did not serve his purposes. Maligning and mistreating people did not affect his conscience at all. He regarded people as objects to help him achieve his own corrupt aims. So let's take a closer look at how the narrator continued to portray Nabal.

As the story unfolded, the festive time of sheep-shearing was at hand, and on such an occasion it was customary to be generous to any neighbors in need.[2] In David's case, they were not only in need but actually performed a protective service for Nabal, perhaps even increasing his profits. Therefore, David sent 10 young men to appeal to Nabal's good nature (not knowing that he did not have one) to provide them with some provisions as charitable payment for performing their flock-guarding services. Conceivably, the size of the party David sent signaled just how much of a gratuity he expected.[3] After their arrival, the men delivered the following gracious message to Nabal from David.

> ...'Have a long life, peace be to you, and peace be to your house, and peace be to all that you have. Now I have heard that you have shearers; now your shepherds have been with us and we have not insulted them, nor have they missed anything all the days they were in Carmel. Ask your young men and they will tell you. Therefore let *my* young men find favor in your eyes, for we have come on a festive day. Please give whatever you find at hand to your servants and to your son David (vv. 6-8).

Dumbfounded could only begin to describe how David's men must have felt when Nabal responded to their request with a vile and insulting rant. I have personally witnessed such outbursts before and felt like curling up in a ball in the corner of a room during the tirade. Here's Nabal's response:

> But Nabal answered David's servants and said, "Who is David? And who is the son of Jesse? There are many servants today who are each breaking away from his master. Shall I then take my bread and my water and my meat that I have slaughtered for my shearers, and give it to men whose origin I do not know" (vv. 10-11)?

Nabal obviously knew who David was. One could infer from the text that his shepherds understood whose band of men was protecting them and their flocks. Nabal's wife, Abigail, knew who David was by attesting that he was to become "ruler over Israel" (v. 30). In the not too distant past, David and his men had rescued the nearby city of Keilah from the Philistines (1 Samuel 23:1-5). David killed Goliath, was a legend, and was loved throughout Israel. With David and his band of 600 men now on the run from Saul, Nabal had to know who David was, and that he was there in his area. So as Nabal uttered, "Who is David? And who is the Son of Jesse?" you could hear the sound of disgust bitterly ringing out in his voice. It was a horrible insult to refuse to acknowledge someone as well-known and important as David. Then Nabal compounded the affront by lumping David and his men together as just a bunch of runaway slaves. Most certainly, it was not a wise thing to say to the anointed one of God. To the affluent and arrogant Nabal, David was a nothing and deserved nothing.

Note how Nabal's self-centeredness came oozing out of his statement in verse 11; "Shall I...take my...and my...and my...that I...for my...whose origin I..." Reminds me of the sea gulls in the Disney movie *Finding Nemo* that incessantly squawk, "Mine, mine, mine." Nabal had an "I" disease that resided in his heart. No gratitude, no love for his neighbor, just a perverted love of self. I wonder what Nabal thought of the commandment to "love your neighbor as yourself" (Leviticus 19:18)? I guess his version left out the middle three words. Remember, we must not only know God's commands but embrace and infuse them into our very being.

Unknown to Nabal, David reacted quite decisively after hearing the wealthy man's offensive response. The wilderness leader said to his men, "Each of you gird on his sword" (v. 13). Four hundred of David's forces now made their way to kill Nabal and all the males on his estate (v. 22).

To further demonstrate Nabal's character, let's look at how others in the story viewed Nabal. Fearing for the lives of everyone involved with Nabal, one of his shepherd's reported to Abigail the unfortunate events in an effort to spur her into action to mitigate the impending calamity. He said,

> Now therefore, know and consider what you should do, for evil is plotted against our master and against all his household; and he is such a worthless man that no one can speak to him (v. 17).

The poor shepherd had probably felt the scorn of Nabal's lips on more than one occasion. Trying to talk sense into a fool was a fruitless endeavor and only ridicule and shame had been the poor shepherd's reward. So, how do those associated with Nabal view him? Worthless. You might think that this shepherd would fear retaliation by referring to his master as "worthless" to his wife. Fortunately, she, more than anyone else, understood and consented to the frantic shepherd's appraisal. After all she was also acquainted with Nabal's brutish tactics. She even verbally validated the shepherd's evaluation of him, when she met up with David, referring to her husband as a "worthless man" as well (v. 25). It's a pretty sad state when you walk around thinking you are "the greatest thing since sliced bread," but everyone else believes you are a heel.

Abigail also knew not to try to reason with her belligerent

husband. When she devised a strategy to save the household and put it into motion, she intentionally "did not tell her husband" (v. 19). No need, since he would have only made a bad situation worse. That's what fools do. When she eventually met up with David, she emphatically told David what a fool Nabal truly was. She said,

> Please do not let my lord pay attention to this worthless man, Nabal, for as his name is, so is he. Nabal is his name and folly is with him…(v. 25).

Yes, Nabal was a fool, and folly followed him wherever he went.

Years ago at NASA, I encountered a "Nabal" in the workforce. This "Nabal" also had power and authority, and he enjoyed making people grovel at his feet. Unfortunately, most people acquiesced to his intimidation as a matter of survival. He enjoyed berating others and embarrassing them in official gatherings. His ways were not always NASA's ways, because he thought he was wiser than everyone else. I actually left one of my positions at NASA because I could not work with this "Nabal." A superior finally understood his foolhardy ways, and he was virtually forced out of the Agency. Most fools' folly eventually catches up with them.

After Nabal sobered up from a drunken stupor, Abigail revealed to her oblivious husband the catastrophe that she had averted with David and his men because of his careless conduct. It is interesting what the storyteller reported next:

> …and his heart died within him so that he became *as* a stone. About ten days later, the Lord struck Nabal and he died (vv. 37-38).

Spiritually, Nabal's heart became hard as a stone many years prior to his physically malady. And as he struck out at God's anointed, Nabal's death came not by the hands of David or from a health-related issue, but by divine judgment administered by God Himself.[4]

Don't ever expect to change the heart of a "Nabal" overnight. Keep in mind the advice of Proverbs: Such people will not listen to your guidance or instruction nor will they follow godly wisdom. Their hearts are aligned with what it takes to achieve their earthly pursuits. Nevertheless, provide them with godly examples, and over time, they may come to realize that your ways produce wonderful fruit, which leads to a more fulfilling and joyful life. And pray for them, because the "Remover of stones" has a history of dealing with the hard-hearted, and in Him there is hope.

> Moreover, I will give you a new heart and put a new spirit within you; and I will remove the heart of stone from your flesh and give you a heart of flesh. I will put My Spirit within you and cause you to walk in My statutes, and you will be careful to observe My ordinances (Ezekiel 36:26).

God will not force this upon anyone, but through Christ Jesus remarkable things can happen, even for a Nabal.

The Shepherd of Shepherds

Several scholars believe that David's pursuit of some kind of compensation for their protection services was objectionable. Basically, the labels of extortionist, terrorist, and shakedown artist have been applied to the future king's activity. As we will discuss in a moment, David did react to Nabal's insulting response in an ungodly manner, but in no way do I believe the text presents David in the light of the above characterizations. David believed that what he had done was "good," and Nabal responded with "evil" (v. 21).

When David sent the ten young men to Nabal, no threats, no show of force, nor the brandishing of weapons is mentioned in the text. In fact, quite the contrary as David sent a gracious blessing to Nabal wishing him and his household "peace...peace... peace" (v. 6). Within David's message, he said that their services were carried out with respect to Nabal's property and shepherds

(v. 7). A point that one of Nabal's own shepherd's confirmed by making the following comment to Abigail.

> Yet the men were very good to us, and we were not insulted, nor did we miss anything as long as we went about with them, while we were in the fields. They were a wall to us both by night and by day, all the time we were with them tending the sheep (1 Samuel 25:15-16).

While on the run from Saul, David protected his fellow countrymen in Keilah from an attack by the Philistines, so why, out of good will, would he not perform these protective services for someone in Maon of Judah? Robert D. Bergen provided an interesting thought on the whole matter. Nabal was introduced in verse three as a Calebite. Bergen points out that not only was the Calebite clan "an esteemed family in Judah," they were "apparently responsible for the founding of David's hometown of Bethlehem (cf. 1 Chronicles 2:51); he [Nabal] was certainly one of David's kinsmen." This viewpoint would explain why David referred to himself as Nabal's "son" at the end of his message (v. 8). David assumed an amicable relationship existed between each other as kinsmen, and therefore provided his services and requested aid in good conscience. Even if you do not hold to this theory, you must admit that David showed humility and respect to Nabal by referring to his men as "servants" to Nabal and to himself as a "son."[5] Obviously, this was not threatening language.

Sheep-shearing season in the Israelite culture was a time of celebration and feasting. Profits from all the hard work were realized, so they celebrated. Since it was also a time of gratitude and benevolence, David acted, per the custom of the day, by sending his men to ask for a handout during this joyous period. In our own culture in the United States, Christmas is a time of giving. Many organizations, like the Salvation Army, petition us for donations. As David looked into the eyes of his hungry men, he sought a donation for his version of a "salvation army."

No doubt if David's troops had been just a bunch of thugs and shakedown artists, they would have taken what they wanted, but David chose to be a good neighbor by performing a vital service for Nabal's shepherds and then asking for what they needed in the proper way.

The truly disturbing aspect of this story was David's reaction to Nabal's demeaning rejection. We are accustomed to the antics of the "Nabals" in this world, so his foolish tirade should come as no surprise. But virtuous heroes like David are expected to act with grace and stay blameless. Yet we see an unimaginable dark side burst forth from him. In the previous chapter, David just mercifully spared Saul's life. The temptation to strike him down must have been overwhelming, as the demented king entered a cave alone, not knowing that David and his men lurked in its dark recesses. David assuredly considered the thought: *I am so tired of running and hiding from this murderous madman, perhaps the time is right for me to end this with one quick thrust of my sword and take the throne that was promised to me.* With his men urging him to strike, David quietly pulled out his sword and could only bring himself to cut off a piece of the king's robe. David's godly trained conscience saved Saul's life and maybe even his own (1 Samuel 24:1-7). In our story, David was instantaneously incited by the words of a fool, and with 400 of his men at his side, he then advanced on Nabal's home, intent on murdering the abusive fool and all of the males in his household (v. 22). What happened to his godly conscience? Was mass murder the answer? Of course with respect to Saul, David highly esteemed God's anointed king, and until God removed him from the throne, David chose to revere him. Was David turning into a Saul? David's rage controlled him, while a veil of bitterness and hate shrouded God from him. The words of Solomon aptly address David's state.

> A stone is heavy and the sand weighty, But the provocation of a fool is heavier than both of them (Proverbs 27:3).

Under the circumstances that faced David, Nabal's words were too weighty for this leader to bear. David's frustrations vehemently poured out as he growled, "Surely in vain I have guarded all that this man has in the wilderness...he has returned me evil for good." Please take a moment and walk in David's shoes. You are running for your life from the king whom you loyally served, removed from your position in the royal family, can no longer experience the comfort of your wife, separated from your friend whose soul was knitted to your own, and your spiritual mentor recently passed away. If that's not enough, you are responsible to seeing for the needs of 600 men and their families while fleeing and hiding out in isolated places. So when the insulting words of a fool are hurled your way, and possibly even bring your choices as a leader into question, the overall weight of this burdensome load causes you to buckle at the knees, and you lose all your composure. Perhaps you can relate. David lost it...really lost it!

Have you ever lost control due to a fool's provocation? In my teen years, I remember our neighborhood "Nabal" getting on my nerves after my team had just lost a game of baseball that we played in a cul-de-sac. Such things were mighty important back in those days. Although I was probably tired and not feeling all that great about losing, "Nabal" bored into me with one of his usual, thoughtless diatribes. Consequently, I momentarily lost my composure. Before I knew it I had thrown two or three punches at him, and he sprawled on the ground. He fell over, not because I hit him, as I was no fighter, he just lost his balance. I then removed myself from his presence so that I could calm down. That response was way out of character for me. I had never thrown a punch at anyone before and haven't since. But is that not a typical reaction when a fool's provocation gets to us? Our circumstances draw us into a weakened state, while rage sits crouching at the door, and when provoked, we lose touch with God and react in sinful ways. That is what I believe David experienced in the extreme. In the next section, we will see how the shepherd of shepherds recovered his composure.

The Wise and Eloquent Maiden

With David on the warpath, the story's hope for a good ending rested with Abigail. The author introduced her in verse three, noting her physical beauty and intelligence. Her beauty, though, was not limited to her appearance. It went to the depths of who she was as a person. Abigail cared about others and had the remarkable ability to project a vision where God takes center-stage in life, while shrewdly addressing one's areas of brokenness. Abigail was a wise and perceptive woman.

Nabal's shepherd convinced Abigail that David meant business…bad business. He anxiously stated, "…for evil is plotted against our master and against all his household" (v. 17). Fortunately, unlike Nabal, Abigail was approachable and fully understood the dire nature of the situation. She immediately formulated a plan to send an extravagant amount of food to David and his men, which more than satisfied the initial request. Abigail and her servants, along with a small train of donkeys packed to the hilt with provisions, made their way to David in an effort to avert the predicament caused by her careless and insensitive husband.

The story provides an interesting detail at this point. Both groups were descending down a mountain on a collision course yet blind to each other's progression. When they suddenly met up, Abigail took advantage of the spontaneity offered by the situation and before David could act, "…she hurried and dismounted from her donkey, and fell on her face before David and bowed herself to the ground" (v. 23). Before a word passed her lips, Abigail humbled herself in an expression of great respect toward Israel's future king. And at his feet in a posture of one pleading for mercy, this remarkable woman delivered one of the most eloquent and wisely crafted speeches we have in God's Word.[6] Note that her words not only sought forgiveness but to calm the infuriated David as well. They also contained a bold, yet subtle, chiding of the young leader.

> "...On me alone, my lord, be the blame. And please let your maidservant speak to you, and listen to the words of your maidservant. Please do not let my lord pay attention to this worthless man, Nabal, for as his name is, so is he. Nabal is his name and folly is with him; but I your maidservant did not see the young men of my lord whom you sent. Now therefore, my lord, as the Lord lives, and as your soul lives, since the Lord has restrained you from shedding blood, and from avenging yourself by your own hand, now then let your enemies and those who seek evil against my lord, be as Nabal. Now let this gift which your maidservant has brought to my lord be given to the young men who accompany my lord. Please forgive the transgression of your maidservant; for the Lord will certainly make for my lord an enduring house, because my lord is fighting the battles of the Lord, and evil will not be found in you all your days. Should anyone rise up to pursue you and to seek your life, then the life of my lord shall be bound in the bundle of the living with the Lord your God; but the lives of your enemies He will sling out as from the hollow of a sling. And when the Lord does for my lord according to all the good that He has spoken concerning you, and appoints you ruler over Israel, this will not cause grief or a troubled heart to my lord, both by having shed blood without cause and by my lord having avenged himself. When the Lord deals well with my lord, then remember your maidservant" (vv. 24-31).

Abigail's humble posture was also portrayed in her words throughout the entire speech. She referred to herself as "maidservant" six times and David as "my lord" 14 times. After imploring David to hear her out and dismissing Nabal as worthless, her words turn into an articulate argument of why he should let go of any vengeance and ill-will toward her household. Let's take a look at a few of the seminal features of her speech.

Right out of the chute, she took the blame. You may be internally thinking, *Sweet Abigail should not take the blame. She did nothing wrong. It was that inconsiderate, stingy Nabal who deserves all the blame!* You're right; he does. However, there is no quicker way to defuse a dicey situation than to take the blame and seek forgiveness, even if you believe you are innocent in the matter. Then, calmer heads will usually prevail, which will promote a civil conversation.

Before Abigail gets into the heart of her argument, she stated that God had already "restrained" him from committing any heinous acts. David could have laid waste to all of them, but his posture and inaction demonstrated that God was at work through this diplomatic woman's words and within David's heart.

Abigail utilized her strategic prowess in selection of some of the words she chose to use. For example, she appealed to David to accept the "gift" of food for his men. The term translated as "gift" means "blessing," and to David's Hebrew ears that had religious overtones. It likely brought the sense that this generous "gift" of food was from God, as He was working through this gracious woman. In other words, this was not a payoff to leave Nabal's family alone, it was a "blessing" from God.[7]

Also, Abigail shrewdly wove into her plea a metaphor of God's using a sling to "sling out" David's enemies. Such a reference assuredly took the giant-killer's mind back to a time when he relied upon God for victory, as he had emphatically claimed to Saul;

> Your servant has killed both the lion and the bear; and this uncircumcised Philistine will be like one of them, since he has taunted the armies of the living God." And David said, "The Lord who delivered me from the paw of the lion and from the paw of the bear, He will deliver me from the hand of this Philistine." And Saul said to David, "Go, and may the Lord be with you" (1 Samuel 17:36-37).

Along with this reference, David's faith in God became a subtle target for wise Abigail. She tactfully pointed out that it was God who restrained Him, God who would give him an enduring house, God who would destroy his enemies, God who promised him the kingship, and God who would appoint him ruler over Israel in due time. Abigail challenged his current intentions in an extraordinary way (my interpretation/words follow), "David, you are trying to chase down a fool, when you are to be 'fighting the battles of the Lord,' so reject evil and let not the guilt of murder be upon you. Too much is at stake for you and Israel, let the role of vengeance remain with the Lord. If you are the anointed one of God…be of God."

One of the most amazing things about this tension-filled scene was that David stopped, listened, and changed his heart. David was fuming mad! Foaming at the mouth mad! Murder vow-making mad and ready to drag 400 men into his folly. How approachable are you in such moments (hopefully not murderous ones, though)? Don't ever think God did not know what He was getting into with David. He knew his vices. But He also was keenly aware that David had a teachable spirit and a heart that sought after His will, even when the fireworks of his humanity temporarily blinded him. Abigail knew how to douse those fireworks and bring this distressed man back in touch with his God. Perhaps David was thinking of Abigail when he poetically developed this comment.

> Let the righteous smite me in kindness and reprove me;
> It is oil upon the head;
> Do not let my head refuse it…
> (Psalms 141:5).

As Abigail liberated David from the blinding turmoil of his rage and opened his eyes to God again, he rallied the courage to discard his anger-fueled vow. Daniel got thrown in the lion's den because of a regrettable vow made by Darius. John the Baptist was beheaded because Herod was too ashamed to go back on the oath he made before his dinner guests. Once David allowed God back into the picture, David had the spiritual means to "eat a little crow" that day and valiantly dismiss his ill-conceived vow. Doing right often takes moral courage when we are surrounded by others who entice us to make wrong choices. Yes, we, too, need an Abigail, at times, to guide us back into God's light.[8]

With his rage and foolish vow behind him, David recovered a thankful heart and made a three-fold blessing, while assuredly looking into the beautiful and relieved eyes of Abigail.

> ..."Blessed be the Lord God of Israel, who sent you this day to meet me, and blessed be your discernment, and blessed be you, who have kept me this day from bloodshed and from avenging myself by my own hand (1 Samuel 25:32-33).

After Nabal died, David married Abigail. That seems like a "wise" thing for the future king to do. One must truly wonder whether Abigail's remarkable discernment provided inspiration for some of his future decisions and the sweet psalmist of Israel's poetry.

Parting Thoughts

Don't expect the "Nabals" of this world to go away anytime soon. You will likely encounter one again; perhaps even today. They may rail on you, make fun of you, lie to you, or take advantage of you. That's what "Nabals" do. Remember, don't turn into a "Nabal" when pounced on by one. Neither is it our calling as Christ's own to despise or mistreat them. In fact, if you detect such attitudes in your heart, you have discovered a spiritual place of brokenness.

When Paul discussed with the church in Rome that they should "never pay back evil for evil to anyone," this included the "Nabals" of the world (Romans 12:17-21). The wise apostle instead instructed them to "overcome evil with good." This involved responding to acts of evil with acts of goodness thus overcoming the evil in others. At the heart of Paul's concern, he was assuredly worried about the spiritual development of the Christians in Rome. Plotting vengeance produces bitter, hateful, and angry hearts; capable of carrying out all sorts of vile deeds. Paul wants us to contemplate on how to respond with goodness, allowing us to develop caring and loving hearts.[9]

If you think God expects a lot, He does! If you don't think pursuing peace, blessing not cursing, refraining from hurtful jabs, and forgiving others is hard enough, please understand what the pinnacle of mature Christianity looks like. You view that hurtful, vile fool with caring eyes. Sin has scarred them deeply, but great potential lies within them in Christ Jesus. So what does God ask of us? He asks us to give them a bottle of water, i.e. assess their needs and respond appropriately with a good deed. Wow, that is hard! They may slap the bottle of water out of our hands, but we need to kindly offer it. Loving your enemies and walking the extra mile with them is tough stuff. And you thought you were spiritually mature! Perhaps you are, but most of us still have a lot of transformative work for God's Spirit to perform in us.

Vengeance is the Lord's! He is not biased, understands all sides, and has an eternal perspective. God's heart is one of pure love, holiness, and goodness and will not be tainted with hate and bitterness. He can handle this heavy load. Leave the vengeance to Him, and get off your throne. Don't expect to always understand His timing. His purposes drive His timing and may have eternal ramifications for others. Let God be God.

David escaped the clutches of vengeance by the gracious speech and actions of Abigail. We all need an "Abigail" in our lives. Seek them out and befriend them, or like David, you may be so fortunate as to marry one. We need their calming influence, sage advice, and for them to come alongside us when hurt and when sorrow intrudes on our world. Restorative power lies within their words. They bring God with them and can help us re-engage with Him. As the world tries to wall off God from us, we need an "Abigail" to help us tear down those walls and open our eyes to His goodness. Let them fill you with a vision of hope, where our God takes center stage in our hearts. And perhaps, you too may become an "Abigail" for someone in need in the future. Yes, even you.

Questions

1. How is Nabal characterized in 1 Samuel 25? Do you know anyone with such a demeanor? How should you act toward them if they mistreat you?

2. Do you believe the story characterizes David as a "shakedown artist?" Explain.

3. David let Nabal's crude response provoke him in a severe way. Were there other factors that might have contributed to David's rage? Have you ever been worked into a frenzy by a "Nabal?" What do you think also contributed to your emotions/anger? How else might you have dealt with the situation?

4. How does the story characterize Abigail? What did Abigail do to calm down David? What did you think were her two most effective tactics and/or parts of her speech?

5. Do you know any "Abigails?" Why is it important for us to all have an "Abigail" in our lives?

6. Why does God want vengeance left to Him?

CHAPTER 2

Ananias and Sapphira
Caught in 'The Acts'

Many will seek the favor of a generous man,
And every man is a friend to him who gives gifts.

(Proverbs 19:6)

Have you ever been blindsided by a perplexing comment? I'll never forget a particular instance when one of my past bosses at NASA left me with a big question mark above my head. I remember going to work one morning and quickly solving a problem that had baffled my colleagues on the previous shift. I speedily resolved the issue because of my familiarity with a particular subsystem, and not because I was more brilliant than my associates. While I was explaining to my coworkers a specific nuance of this subsystem, my boss stood in the background intently listening to what I had to say. As I concluded, he suddenly took a couple steps closer to our group and blurted out, "O'Neal, you are a pin-taper!" Extremely confused, I turned and looked at him with a puzzled expression on my face and replied, "What?!?" He then started laughing. He was fully aware that he would confound me with such a bizarre remark. Even though he was "just joking," he then explained by revealing an alarming and serious event from his past. My boss was a world-class storyteller and "doozy" only begins to describe the true story that he shared.

In a previous program, a particular engineer/technician was a legend for his efficient troubleshooting that resulted in the expeditious resolution of problems related to one of the key ground control systems. During major activities, when a malfunction occurred on this complicated hardware, he often promptly "swooped" in and discovered the source of the dilemma and made the necessary corrections. Then able to continue with the day's important endeavor, the team always applauded his heroic efforts. However, one day this "star" fell back to Earth. In advance of an upcoming activity, he surmised that a particular electronic function would be required. After identifying which circuit board was responsible for this function, the "supposed" hero then pulled it out of its electronics chassis. He proceeded to wrap tape around one of the board's pins, and then carefully reinserted it back into its connector, therefore disabling its capability. When the hardware experienced an anomaly due to his devious tactics, he knew right where to go to find and fix the problem. Fortunately, his fraudulent scheme was discovered, and he faced serious repercussions for his actions.

Why would someone become a "pin-taper?" One can only infer what his rationale was, but surely the accolades, awards, and potential promotions provided the enticement for him to lower himself to such devious scheming. You have probably witnessed a contemptible act by a self-promoter in your life, since it is an age-old vice. In fact, we have a documented case in God's Word of a couple of Christians in the early church who fell prey to its egocentric lure.

Life in the Early Jerusalem Church

Shortly after the Pentecost that followed Christ's Ascension, the church in Jerusalem grew rapidly, as the gospel quickly spread. Often when groups experience a sudden surge in numbers, chaos and disharmony can result because of ill-preparedness to handle such an unexpected change. Nonetheless, this Spirit-driven community of believers maintained a remarkable unity.

Luke provided us with the following summary of life within the Jerusalem church during this timeframe.

> And the congregation of those who believed were of one heart and soul; and not one *of them* claimed that anything belonging to him was his own, but all things were common property to them. And with great power the apostles were giving testimony to the resurrection of the Lord Jesus, and abundant grace was upon them all. For there was not a needy person among them, for all who were owners of land or houses would sell them and bring the proceeds of the sales and lay them at the apostles' feet, and they would be distributed to each as any had need (Acts 4:32-35).

What a wonderful blessing it must have been to be a part of a body of Christians where peace, harmony, and care for one another reigned despite transitional difficulties.

Congregations undergoing discord and disunity lose their focus on what is truly important. Rather than giving attention to leading others to Christ, nurturing their membership, and stimulating good works, the leadership and ministry team sometimes become sidetracked (and often entangled) with brothers and sisters who are bickering over methodologies, self-centered preferences, and other divisive issues. Obviously, such an environment can become toxic and not conducive to accomplishing any of the church's core purposes. For those of us who have gone through such turbulent times, we can tell you that you yearn for the type of peace and harmony that existed at the Jerusalem church.

When believers live together in the oneness of "heart and soul," God can accomplish extraordinary things through and within His people. In such an atmosphere, the Spirit's transformative work of developing sacrificial givers can be more readily achieved. The intertwining of unity and love for others facilitates our embracing and carrying out an important teaching of Jesus: "It is more blessed to give than to receive" (Acts 20:35). The Jerusalem church provides a historic example of what can be realized when such harmony exists.

Prior to Jesus' arrest and crucifixion, He prayed for those who would believe in Him through the apostles' teaching. This request of His Father has profound implications for us today.

> I do not ask on behalf of these alone, but for those also who believe in Me through their word; that they may all be one; even as You, Father, *are* in Me and I in You, that they also may be in Us, so that the world may believe that You sent Me (John 17:20-21).

When a congregation's oneness becomes so strikingly obvious to the world, the words of the gospel preacher become more powerful and persuasive. Witnessing true unity among believers, aids the hearer in recognizing that God "sent" Jesus into the world to redeem humankind. Along with the Spirit-derived boldness and abilities of the apostles (ref. Acts 4:30-31), the attractiveness of God's people thriving in a pleasing harmony contributed to the "great power" that accompanied their testimony of the resurrected Christ. Their testimony resulted in "multitudes of men and women" turning to Jesus for salvation (Acts 5:14).

Luke decided to leave us with a tangible example of the sacrificial love that was experienced in the Jerusalem church by introducing Barnabas for the first time in his beloved book.

> Now Joseph, a Levite of Cyprian birth, who was also called Barnabas by the apostles (which translated means Son of Encouragement), and who owned a tract of land, sold it and brought the money and laid it at the apostles' feet (Acts 4:36-37).

Some of the converts who had ventured to Jerusalem for Pentecost assuredly remained to gain from the apostles' teachings. Their resources would have become depleted because of the prolonged trip. Along with this problem, the local Jews who decided to follow Christ faced financial ruin by their former brethren, as they would avoid doing business with those associated with this "fringe" element of their religion. The young Jerusalem church was challenged by a true economic emergency and needed help from within its developing ranks. With the opportunity to learn sacrificial giving at hand, some of the members of this fledgling group gave in such an amazing and selfless way that "there was not a needy person among them" (v. 34).

We may ask, "Why was Barnabas singled out, when obviously a number of others were involved in this good work?" Maybe Luke chose to use this incident to introduce an upcoming key character of his book, which it nobly accomplished. Barnabas's gift possibly exceeded the others in value, though the text does not indicate that this was the case. Perhaps Luke included this example because it contributed to the unfolding story of the Jerusalem church. Not only was his gift exemplary, it, along with other gracious deeds, earned him the acclaimed name, "Son of Encouragement," a title coveted by another.

An Ugly Black Eye

Significant moral failures in life tend to leave a glaring black eye—one that no makeup can hide. That black and blue swollen abnormality serves as a magnet to attract gaze after gaze from even a remote observer. Whether caught in a lie, crime, or some other scandalous activity, the pervasiveness of the resulting shame makes it too hard to cover up. It is truly noteworthy that God has not tried to whitewash the mistakes of the Bible's heroes of faith. In God's Word, their celebrated successes stand alongside the ugliness of their shortcomings and failures. Abraham, the father of faith, did not trust God for deliverance, but turned to deceit on two occasions (Genesis 12:10-20; 20). Moses, who led God's people out of Egypt, disregarded God's instructions in one instance, which was tantamount to not treating Him as holy, and he was kept from entering the Promised Land (Numbers 20:8-13). David, the sweet psalmist of Israel and a man after God's own heart, committed adultery and murder (2 Samuel 11). Peter, a pillar of the Christian faith, denied that he knew Jesus three times (Luke 22:54-62). Even God's chosen people, the Hebrews, were so disobedient in their pursuit of idols and other sinful activities that God allowed them to be conquered and led away in captivity. Why did God allow these black eyes to persist through the ages for us to plainly see? I sincerely believe these stories reside in all their ugliness to thoroughly demonstrate that we need Him. He dearly loves us, and we so desperately need Him.

As Luke continued to unfold the story of the first-century church in Jerusalem, we encounter a horrible black eye that would forever blemish this idyllic church. Many reasons may exist for why Luke included the tragic account of Ananias and Sapphira's misdeeds, but we should remember that no church is perfect. Churches are filled with imperfect people—people who desperately need God's grace, the forgiveness found in Christ's blood, and the transformative power of God's Spirit. Even though this narrative's tragic conclusion bewilders our modern-day conscience, be thankful for its inclusion in our sacred text, because we can learn much from this disastrous story.

> But a man named Ananias, with his wife Sapphira, sold a piece of property, and kept back *some* of the price for himself, with his wife's full knowledge, and bringing a portion of it, he laid it at the apostles' feet. But Peter said, "Ananias, why has Satan filled your heart to lie to the Holy Spirit and to keep back *some* of the price of the land? While it remained *unsold*, did it not remain your own? And after it was sold, was it not under your control? Why is it that you have conceived this deed in your heart? You have not lied to men but to God." And as he heard these words, Ananias fell down and breathed his last; and great fear came over all who heard of it. The young men got up and covered him up, and after carrying him out, they buried him. Now there elapsed an interval of about three hours, and his wife came in, not knowing what had happened. And Peter responded to her,

"Tell me whether you sold the land for such and such a price?" And she said, "Yes, that was the price." Then Peter *said* to her, "Why is it that you have agreed together to put the Spirit of the Lord to the test? Behold, the feet of those who have buried your husband are at the door, and they will carry you out *as well*." And immediately she fell at his feet and breathed her last, and the young men came in and found her dead, and they carried her out and buried her beside her husband. And great fear came over the whole church, and over all who heard of these things (Acts 5:1-11).

This dreadful incident is attached to the preceding summary of life in the Jerusalem church via the conjunction *but*. This *but* brutally intruded on a beautiful story. We would prefer an *and* that continued with a description of the loving, faith-filled accomplishments of this serene church. Yet we are given a *but*. This could be reminiscent of your church. You might profess, "Our church is so loving, *but* we recently had to let our preacher go because it was discovered that he was addicted to pornography." "Our church's members are extraordinary givers, *but* our treasurer was caught embezzling money from our accounts." "Our church is so service-oriented, *but* several families recently left because they disagreed with some of the recent changes instituted by our leadership." On and on we could go…*buts* are a reality of church life. They will continue to impose themselves even on *good* congregations. Yes, the church needs its Lord—desperately!

We may want to consider that Ananias and Sapphira were two bad eggs from the beginning in an otherwise righteous church. However, Luke was emphatic that the congregation was "of one heart and soul" (Acts 4:32). Were not Ananias and Sapphira part of this congregation? Surely Luke included them when he claimed that "not one of them" viewed their belongings as their own. So what transpired in this couple's heart that caused them to depart from the wonderful principles their congregation practiced?

What Ananias and Sapphira did was despicable, but before we start throwing stones at them, let's take a few things into consideration. Remember, they were young Christians. Their hearts were in an early phase of development. Some deeply rooted vices may not have yet surfaced and been addressed. Their hearts and minds were potentially shaped by a common practice in the ancient Mediterranean world, where benefactors expected public honor for showing their good will.[10] Surely we can relate. Immediately following our own conversion, though we were forgiven and counted as holy, God's Spirit had considerable transformative work to accomplish within us over the years to come. Sometimes deeply held attitudes instilled by our experiences and culture don't change easily. And as immature Christians go, Ananias and Sapphira may not have been that much different than many of us.

A Potential Scenario

To better understand what occurred in the hearts and minds of this couple, let's look at a potential scenario based on the information given that would help explain the outcome. Try to imagine yourself in the Jerusalem church during this time period. You see that many of your brothers and sisters are suffering and need help. Your heart goes out to them, and you want to address their needs in some way. Some of your number have sold a portion of their possessions and brought substantial sums of money to the apostles to distribute to those in need. Even though these extravagant gifts were voluntary, this still places a considerable amount of pressure on you to do the same, since you own a piece of land that you could sell. Nevertheless, you want to help, so you and your spouse seriously consider selling the land and contributing the proceeds.

In response to some of the more sizeable donations, you overhear some of your brothers and sisters highly praising these benevolent givers. Some of their comments start to tickle your ears, such as, "Wow, what a generous couple!" "Brother Andrew is such a good Christian man." "Sister Lydia sure has a wonderful heart." You even hear the apostles start calling your friend, Joseph, by a new nickname— "Barnabas," i.e. "the son of encouragement." On hearing these accolades, something starts to stir in your heart. You strongly desire such praise as well. Envy begins to displace the desire to help others with a longing to be admired by your fellow Christians. Now driven by envious yearnings, you decide to sell your property.

Let's consider the character trait of envy for a moment. Envy is a powerful motivator. Envy cherishes and desperately wants what another person possesses. Whether a title, position, money, car, home, good looks, charisma, or whatever you admire...you want it. You crave it to such an extreme that you start to resent the person who has these things or qualities. Envy powered by an agonizing discontentment begins to direct your behaviors in contemptible ways. You callously plot and manipulate circumstances and others to obtain your heart's envious desires.

A minister once shared with me how envy overtook him on a couple of occasions. He was between jobs and attending a church that some of his friends recommended. Experiencing his Christianity from an unfamiliar vantage point, the unemployed minister intently listened to the preacher's sermons from the pews. He knew he should use this time to enrich his spirituality, but an unfamiliar attitude took hold of him. He started to critique the sermons, developing different ways to handle the topics—and in a "superior" way. Envy started to creep into his heart, as he imagined himself up in the pulpit delivering a "better-quality" message. In his mind he thought, *These folks do not know what they are missing.* As he actually started to feel a tinge of resentment toward his interim congregation's preacher, he came to his senses. Some dark thoughts intruded on his soul, but he fortunately caught them in time and addressed these loathsome attitudes before he said or did something he would surely regret.

Back to our "potential" scenario: Your property has sold for a considerable amount of money. Pleased to no end, you cannot wait to hear how everyone will applaud your efforts and generosity. You will be the talk of the church. And oh yes, it will help those in need as well. What once was truly honorable, the sacrificial giving to help others has now become a secondary motivator in your heart. As you continue salivating over the honor you will receive, your eyes suddenly shift down to the pile of money sitting on your table. You start to think, *Wow, that is a lot of cash!* You earnestly express to your wife, "We sure could use some of this to make that addition to our home we've been wanting." "Perhaps we should set some of this aside to help us live more comfortably as we age. You know what, Sapphira, I have always wanted to give you a fine piece of jewelry, like John gave his wife, to demonstrate my love for you." Greed subtly creeps into your heart, and you start to covet some of this money once earmarked for others.

Regrettably, a tragic battle from your people's heritage has faded from your memory with its invaluable application to your current situation. During the conquest of the land of Canaan, your Hebrew ancestors were easily laying waste to the pagan cities of this territory as directed by God. Although, when they came up against the city of Ai, Israel suffered a sounding defeat. God said the reason for their failure was because the covenant had been broken with Him concerning the spoils of war; they had "taken some of the things under the ban and have both stolen and deceived" (Joshua 7:11). Not only was this a transgression of the covenant, God viewed it as a "disgraceful thing" (v. 15). When Joshua confronted Achan on this matter, the guilty Judean made the following confession.

...'Truly, I have sinned against the Lord, the God of Israel, and this is what I did: when I saw among the spoil a beautiful mantle from Shinar and two hundred shekels of silver and a bar of gold fifty shekels in weight, then I coveted them and took them; and behold, they are concealed in the earth inside my tent with the silver underneath it' (v. 20-21).

Surely, Achan's initial intent was to follow God's commands and nobly fight alongside his countrymen. Taking advantage of the spoils of war was probably not something he desired or contemplated. Achan's fall came when the situation confronted him. He "saw" and "then" "coveted." Like David seeing Bathsheba bathing on an adjacent rooftop, he "saw" and *then coveted* (2 Samuel 11:2-4). Certainly his rooftop venture did not come with the expectation of lusting after one of his mighty men's wives. Yet, when confronted with an alluring temptation—he "saw" and "saw" and "saw." We, too, may enter into a given situation with the best of intentions, but when we "see" that is when the coveting starts. Jesus said,

'The eye is the lamp of the body; so then if your eye is clear, your whole body will be full of light. But if your eye is bad, your whole body will be full of darkness. If then the light that is in you is darkness, how great is the darkness!' (Matthew 6:22-23)

When Achan "saw" and when David "saw," an area of weakness (or darkness) rose up inside them, and they did not have the spiritual resources to fight off the roaring flames of temptation. Remember my friends, ask God to lay bare your weaknesses before your eyes so that you can address them with Him; perhaps with a close confidant by your side as well. Expose any darkness within you with the true light of God's Word. While you press on to spiritual maturity, you will become more spiritually resilient to deal with any underlying weaknesses that remain within you.

So as you stand there *scrutinizing* all that loot, greed overtakes you and spawns a covetous and unscrupulous scheme that allows you to not only receive the accolades you so fondly desire but also to keep a large portion of the money. You will deceive the apostles and your congregation by giving only a portion of the money, while insinuating that it is the entire amount for the property you sold. As you approach Peter to lay the money at his feet, you are pleased with your shrewdness, yet an unsettling feeling comes over you. Too bad it did not preclude what you proceeded to say.

The Outcome

Our 21st-century Christian sentiments desire and expect mercy and grace in this story's outcome. Tragically, death came swiftly for this scheming couple by divine judgment and intervention. Why so serious a verdict? Was not the transgression precipitated by some common character flaws? Peter emphatically gave us the answer by stating it in three different ways in this short narrative: Ananias told a "lie to the Holy Spirit" (v. 3); he "lied to...God" (v. 4); and they "...put the Spirit of the Lord to the test" (v. 9). Even though it was true that God's Spirit dwelt within Ananias and Sapphira (1 Corinthians 6:19), I do not believe this directly influenced the harsh judgment. Up to this point in Acts, the members of the Jerusalem church had witnessed "many wonders and signs" through the Spirit-empowered apostles (Acts 2:43). God was present in this congregation like at no other point in church history, as He divinely worked in and through the apostles in miraculous ways to guide and facilitate their early successes. With Peter able to divinely determine the intention of Ananias and Sapphira's hearts, their lies "tested" Peter's empowerment, or in other words, the Spirit's ability to appraise him of their sordid ways. When they lied to Peter, they lied to God.

What Else Went Wrong

Along with the several and aforementioned unfortunate aspects of this story other features of this event insinuate a few more things went very wrong. For one, Ananias and Sapphira were a Christian couple. Assuming that Ananias pulled his wife into this appalling ruse, we must ask ourselves why she didn't protest his misguided idea. We are not given the intricate details to all that occurred, but it appears that neither one questioned the other's motives. Neither one noted the unsavory character traits at work. Neither pointed out the un-Christian behavior. Neither felt concerned about the deceit. Neither seemed to worry about the possibility of the apostles' uncovering their scam.

One of the many wonderful aspects about a Christian marriage is that it can serve as a check and balance to questionable behavior. Throughout our marriage, I have not been immune to some bad attitudes and conduct at times, and my wife has shown a lot of patience with me during those periods. However, when they turned destructive, she quickly intervened, letting me know about her concerns with my ill-conceived thinking and/or ways. On most of these occasions, she became pretty direct, but a couple of times, she had to wake me up by hitting me between the eyes with a two-by-four (metaphorically speaking, of course). Nevertheless, our communication lines remained open to pass along this sorely needed advice. For Ananias and Sapphira, however, not only did this horrendously fail in their marriage, but they actually supported one another in their subversion.

Another aspect to the story worth noting is that Peter provided Sapphira with an opportunity to correct the wrong. Not knowing that her husband had dropped dead at the apostle's feet just a few hours earlier, Peter implored of her: "Tell me whether you sold the land for such and such a price" (Acts 5:8). She easily could have cleared the air at that moment by repenting and confessing of the wrongdoing. Desiring a partially good ending, we want to yell back through the centuries and plead, "Tell the truth, Sapphira, and receive mercy!" Regrettably, she continued the charade and told another bold-faced lie. Peter tested her; she "tested" the Spirit; she failed. Hearts caught up in sin are hard to penetrate, but let's never stop trying.

Lastly, Satan entered the scene. Luke provided a startling contrast concerning the spiritual activity within the Jerusalem church. On one hand, he noted that some were "filled with the Holy Spirit" (Acts 4:31) after an energizing prayer. Then Luke reported Peter's response to Ananias, "Why has Satan filled your heart to lie to the Holy Spirit…" (Acts 5:3). God fills His believers to spread the truth of the gospel; Satan fills hearts to deceive.[11] Honorably, Ananias could have reported that he only gave a portion of the money, while keeping back some for personal needs. That was a perfectly acceptable and praiseworthy solution. But envy and greed distorted his thinking and provided Satan an opening. The Father of Lies provided a deceitful solution that allowed Ananias to take full credit and the resulting praise for something that was not due to him. Please understand, Peter directly placed the blame on Ananias' shoulders when he said, "Why is it that *you* have conceived this deed in your heart?" (v. 4) (Emphasis is mine.). Satan may desire to fill, but we must first open our hearts.[12] Never give Satan an opportunity. Guard those hearts!

Parting Thoughts

We live in a culture of discontentment. Media political pundits constantly try to create dissatisfaction with one party's positions or their elected officials. Sports talk shows stir up strife over a coach's record and decisions. Many commercials are unashamedly designed to make you feel unhappy with your appearance. Social media trolls spew venomous gossip and hate-filled speech about others. You can add to the list; it will be a long one. What is their goal? They want to create a state of discontentment within you, one that lives and breathes and leads you to act in some form or fashion. A discontented spirit is a gloomy, restless existence where peace is forever fleeting.

While driving home from work years ago, I used to listen to

political talk radio quite a bit. Of course, the hosts on these shows incessantly try to make you feel discontented about an opposing party's piece of legislation or idea. I remember often being so flustered by the time I arrived home that I was ready to bite someone's head off rather than be a loving father and husband. I came to the realization that listening to such programs all the time was not good for me because of the unrelenting angst it produced in me. I still garner some opinions from them now and then, but I now typically listen to programming that produces a more positive frame-of-mind. Many of you have probably had similar experiences.

Well, what's wrong with a little discontentment? Sometimes it can bring about some unhealthy attitudes and behaviors. In the case of Ananias and Sapphira, I believe discontentment lay at the core of their demise. Seeing others praised had an unsettling effect on this pair that produced an intense envy for the same. Not content with their current lifestyle, greed with all of its toxicity grabbed hold of them, as they viewed that stack of money. A contented heart does not seek accolades, but gladly praises the accomplishments of others. A contented heart is at peace with one's financial status and joyously and generously gives when needs arise. The author of Hebrews made this vital comment concerning contentment.

> *Make sure that* your character is free from the love of money, being content with what you have; for He Himself has said, "I will never desert you, nor will I ever forsake you," so that we confidently say, "The Lord is my helper, I will not be afraid. What will man do to me" (Hebrews 13:5-6).

Contentment never comes from pursuing money. Contentment fully takes root when we trust in God's provision and presence and faithfully believe that He "is my helper." Actually, placing an undue emphasis on money creates a restless spirit and a basic distrust of God's provisional care for His people.[13]

Many Christians struggle with the love of money. They're not satisfied with what they have and continually seek ways to increase their assets. Secretive and inconspicuous tactics to achieve this goal are especially seductive for Christians who struggle with this insidious vice. The following are a few examples. The "lover of money" may record additional hours on their timesheets that they did not work. They report on their income taxes more donations than they actually gave. They take back an item to a store after they used it, claiming it is still new. They secretly bring home office supplies from work, avoiding buying them with their own money. In all of these cases, the love of money produced lying, stealing, cheating, and lawbreaking, along with the devious planning that it took to carry out these acts. God wants His people's thought-world to focus on how to help others, not to be mired in selfish pursuits. Achieving such an approach to life will root out discontentment, because our emphasis will be on others as God intends.

When Paul made his acclaimed statement to the Philippians that he had "learned to be content in whatever circumstances" he encountered (Philippians 4:11), it was basically a faith statement to his trust in God. His contentment came from His dependence on God, and as such, circumstances, people, money, and things did not define or sway him. God did. When you arrive at such a place in life, you can then say as Paul did, "I can do all things through Him who strengthens me" (v. 13). He found contentment; so can we.

So how did Paul arrive there? I find it interesting that just prior to Paul's claim of contentment to the Philippians, he encouraged them to do the following:

> Rejoice in the Lord always; again I will say, rejoice! Let your gentle *spirit* be known to all men. The Lord is near. Be anxious for nothing, but in everything by prayer and supplication with thanksgiving let your requests be made known to God. And the

peace of God, which surpasses all comprehension, will guard your hearts and your minds in Christ Jesus.

Finally, brethren, whatever is true, whatever is honorable, whatever is right, whatever is pure, whatever is lovely, whatever is of good repute, if there is any excellence and if anything worthy of praise, dwell on these things. The things you have learned and received and heard and seen in me, practice these things, and the God of peace will be with you (Philippians 4:4-9).

I believe Paul's contentment was produced by these very practices, so he wanted to pass these along to help them achieve this desired state of being as well.

Let's take a look at Paul's approach to achieving peace. First, rejoice in what God has done for you in Christ Jesus. He's redeemed and forgiven you. You are an adopted son or daughter to the ultimate Father. Your relationship with Him is grounded in His love for you. He has placed His Spirit within you. You have the hope of spending eternity with Him. And there are many more reasons we can list to rejoice. So yes, rejoice—always!

Second, we should have forbearing and gentle spirits toward others. You need to be patient with them as they grow. When they fall, you should help them spiritually heal and constructively learn from their mistakes. Forgive others when you are wronged, not allowing their indiscretions to stir up vengeful feelings inside you. Like Paul said, as "far as it depends on you, be at peace with all men" and "overcome evil with good" (Romans 12:18, 21).

Third, when life makes you anxious, take it to the Lord in prayer. Tell Him about your money concerns, your ambition for a promotion at work, and the envy that overtakes you because of what others possess. Express your requests in all thankfulness for what He has done and is doing in your life. He is a gracious, trustworthy, and holy God, who loves us dearly, and we need to express our appreciation to Him. Prayer is an act of trust in God, so pray believing that He will act as He promises. And what is

His promise? He will provide you with peace. His peace! And for that reason, you may not understand it. God perceives things differently than we do, and from his vantage point, He has the ability to turn your anxiousness into something that is not so unsettling. Gordon D. Fee astutely suggests the following: "Peace comes because prayer is an expression of trust, and God's people do not need to have it all figured out in order to trust Him!"[14]

God's peace yields contentment, and as such, it protects our hearts and minds. Where our anxiety produces discontentment that leads to sinful attitudes, the peace of God now promotes contentment and a godly approach to our life's circumstances.

To reinforce God's peace, Paul encouraged dwelling on the good things of life. Stop allowing life's negative aspects to consume your thought-world; focus on what is admirable. What does all the negative bring about? Anxiety and discontentment! What does the positive bring about? Peace and contentment! What's your choice?

Lastly, Paul urged them to practice the Christian principles that they had learned from him, and by walking in such a sound manner "the God of peace shall be with you." Yes, He is with you, because He is in you. And of all that luscious fruit He produces inside of you, let *peace* (Galatians 5:22) bring forth a bountiful life of contentment, knowing that you can join Paul in saying that "I can do all things through Him who strengthens me."

Questions

1. How do unity and oneness help produce growth in a church? How might you contribute to your congregation's unity?

2. God has revealed to us in His Word some of the unsavory aspects of His people, along with their many positive accomplishments. Why do you think this is the case?

3. Why do you believe Ananias and Sapphira acted like they did?

What drove their behaviors? Have you ever experienced any of these inner attitudes? Do they still present a problem for you at times? How might you deal with them?

4. Explain what *envy* and *greed* are and how they work in us humans.

5. How does discontentment contribute to our negative character traits?

6. Do you have any areas of discontentment in your life? How might you move to a more contented lifestyle?

7. Of what do you think the peace of God consists? How are peace and contentment related?

CHAPTER 3

Shimei

Faith and Stone Throwers

**Fools give full vent to their rage,
but the wise bring calm in the end.**

(Proverbs 29:11)

S ome chemicals when mixed together are quite volatile. NASA astutely takes advantage of this property in many of their propulsion systems. On the Space Shuttle Orbiter, the Orbital Maneuvering System (OMS) engines and Reaction Control System (RCS) thrusters use hypergolic propellants, which ignite spontaneously on contact with one another (no spark required). The two OMS engines were used for orbit insertion, orbit circularization, orbit transfer, rendezvous, deorbit, and in some abort scenarios. These engines were your workhorses while in space. For smaller movements, the RCS thrusters did the trick. So to move the Orbiter in a specific direction or change its attitude, you fired the required thrusters. Not that the Orbiters had "attitude" problems like us humans, but sometimes NASA needed to reorient them to accomplish the task at hand. To fire one of these engines, the fuel and oxidizer propellants were allowed to flow into their combustion chamber, and since they were hypergolic, the liquids ignited on contact. The hot gases were then expanded through a nozzle to propel the Orbiter in the desired direction; relatively slow, of course, for the RCS thrusters.

As you might imagine, a lot of safeguards must be put in place in order to design systems that use hypergolic propellants. Not only do these commodities combust on contact with each other, they are also lethal. At the Kennedy Space Center, the fuel and oxidizer depots were located on opposite sides of the launch pad from one another for the Shuttle Program. If a major leak occurred, you by no means wanted these propellants in close proximity to one another, since a dangerous explosion might occur that could seriously damage the launch pad and the Space Shuttle, and possibly even result in the loss of life.

You probably know of a few individuals or families that are "hypergolic." They combust on contact with one another. We will investigate, what I believe, is one such situation during the time of David, and I think you will see some deep-seated animosity that existed between one family and their king.

An Odd Outburst

When it comes to bizarre stories, God's Word contains its fair share. In fact, you probably have a favorite; it's hard to beat a talking donkey, though. The next story is rather odd, too, and it begs the question about why God chose to pass it along to us. Whatever the case, we can learn some valuable lessons from this strange story.

Late in David's life, his son, Absalom, led a rebellion against his father's rule and took over the kingdom. In 2 Samuel 16, David is in the midst of fleeing from Jerusalem with an entourage consisting of his family, servants, some loyal foreign warriors, and his mighty men. David could not help but weep and cover his head as he sadly left the capital city that he had founded not so many years ago (2 Samuel 15:30). His world was collapsing in on him, and he knew that he bore the responsibility for the bitter happenings he was facing. After committing adultery with Bathsheba and staging her husband's death in a battle with the Ammonites, David took the pregnant widow for his wife

(2 Samuel 11). David's cover up may have eluded the notice of his subjects, but God sorrowfully looked on as the out-of-control king concocted and carried out the whole sinful charade. God not only viewed David's deeds as evil, but such heinous acts truly demonstrated that he "despised" God Himself and His Word (2 Samuel 12:9-10). Sin always has its costs, and for David, the price was steep. So as David abruptly fled Jerusalem, the harrowing reality of two of God's decrees unfolded before him. God told him that "the sword shall never depart from your house," and that "I will raise up evil against you from your own household" (2 Samuel 12:10-11). David's burdens were great. He not only sinned against the God whom he trusted and owed his successes, but one of his beloved sons wanted to take his life. With each step, the memories of failure placed a heavy load on the sweet psalmist of Israel. Perhaps it was along this road of despair that David started to develop the deep thoughts and feelings he shared in Psalm 51. David's desperation for God to restore some sort of peace in his life is readily evident in the following excerpt from this powerful psalm.

> Make me to hear joy and gladness,
> Let the bones which You have broken rejoice.
> Hide Your face from my sins
> And blot out all my iniquities.
> Create in me a clean heart, O God,
> And renew a steadfast spirit within me.
> Do not cast me away from Your presence
> And do not take Your Holy Spirit from me.
> Restore to me the joy of Your salvation
> And sustain me with a willing spirit.
> ...Deliver me from bloodguiltiness,
> O God, the God of my salvation;
> *Then* my tongue will joyfully sing
> of Your righteousness (vv. 8-12, 14).

You probably remember shouting as a child, "do-over!" as you made a detrimental mistake in a game you were playing. Or similarly, you have witnessed a quarterback throw a costly interception, yet one of the referees threw a penalty flag during the play. As a camera zooms in on the quarterback, you note that his gaze was anxiously locked in on the referees as they quickly huddled together, hoping their ruling will go against the other team, so he could run the play over. Actual life, however, does not come with many "do-overs." When we make mistakes, we should be accountable, repent, ask for forgiveness, and trust God to mercifully help us through any troubling consequences.

As David and his careworn band made their way to the fords of the Jordan River, they went by the Benjamite village of Bahurim. Out of nowhere, a raving lunatic decided to unload a lot of pent-up hostility on David. Separated by a narrow valley, the crazed man stood cursing on a hillside opposite David's group as they progressed along the roadway.[15] Let's look closer at this unusual scene.

> When King David came to Bahurim, behold, there came out from there a man of the family of the house of Saul whose name was Shimei, the son of Gera; he came out cursing continually as he came. He threw stones at David and at all the servants of King David; and all the people and all the mighty men were at his right hand and at his left. Thus Shimei said when he cursed, "Get out, get out, you man of bloodshed, and worthless fellow! The Lord has returned upon you all the bloodshed of the house of Saul, in whose place you have reigned; and the Lord has given the kingdom into the hand of your son Absalom. And behold, you are *taken* in your own evil, for you are a man of bloodshed!"

> Then Abishai the son of Zeruiah said to the king, "Why should this dead dog curse my lord the king? Let me go over now and cut off his head." But the king said, "What have I to do with you, O sons of Zeruiah? If he curses, and if the Lord has told him, 'Curse David,' then who shall say, 'Why have you done so?'"

Then David said to Abishai and to all his servants, "Behold, my son who came out from me seeks my life; how much more now this Benjamite? Let him alone and let him curse, for the Lord has told him. Perhaps the Lord will look on my affliction and return good to me instead of his cursing this day." So David and his men went on the way; and Shimei went along on the hillside parallel with him and as he went he cursed and cast stones and threw dust at him (2 Samuel 16:5-13).

Irony tends to unleash itself in uncanny ways and at traumatic moments. David's rise to power in Saul's ranks came with the aid of a stone slung so hard by a lone young shepherd that it penetrated a Philistine giant's forehead, which rallied Saul's troops to rout the dreaded Philistine army (1 Samuel 17). Now, a lone man from the house of Saul took aim at the Goliath-slayer. His stones were not thrown with a force to penetrate a forehead, but to strike a humiliating blow deep into the human spirit.

At the core of Shimei's cursing was the accusation that David was a murderer ("man of bloodshed"), and he stood guilty of "all the bloodshed of the house of Saul." To what was Shimei specifically referring? To whose deaths within Saul's house was he drawing attention? First, Shimei was probably blaming David for the death of Saul and Jonathan. You may ask, "Did not David love Jonathan" (2 Samuel 1:26)? "Did he not respect and care deeply for Saul, God's anointed king?" "Did he not prevent some of his men from killing crazed Saul on a couple of occasions" (1 Samuel 24:1-7, 26:8-9). "Was it not the Philistines who killed Saul and Jonathan" (1 Samuel 31:1-6)? "Did not David tearfully mourn their deaths" (2 Samuel 1:1-12, 17-27)? We must remember, at the time of Saul and Jonathan's deaths, David was allied with and living among the Philistines. Even though he did not go into battle against Israel and contribute to the king and prince's deaths, Saul's relatives may have believed otherwise. It was certainly reasonable for them to assume that David was a traitor, and as such, played a role in the death of the king. Shimei actually hinted at David's responsibility for Saul's death, when he held him accountable for "all the bloodshed of the house of Saul" and then disdainfully added, "in whose place you have reigned" (v. 8).

Second, another flawed belief may have ruled the day concerning the deaths of Ish-bosheth, Saul's only surviving son, and Abner, Saul's general and cousin.[16] As a successor to Saul, Abner had Ish-bosheth crowned king over Israel (2 Samuel 2:6-9). Again, we know that Joab killed Abner (2 Samuel 3:27), and two of Ish-bosheth's own commanders killed him in his sleep (2 Samuel 4). Nevertheless, Saul's household may have believed that David was responsible and had commissioned both murders. Such a move would have been viewed as politically expedient and shrewd, aiding David in his aspirations to take over the entire kingdom. Conspiracy theories are not a modern phenomenon.

Third, Saul's relatives surely blamed David for handing over seven of Saul's descendants to the Gibeonites, which resulted in their deaths (2 Samuel 21). Saul viewed the Gibeonites with contempt during his reign and sought to "exterminate" (v. 5) any of them within the borders of Israel. By doing so, Saul broke the covenant that Joshua made with them (Joshua 9:15-19), and they demanded justice in some form. So they requested that David turn over to them "seven men from" Saul's sons (v. 6). David obliged, and they were subsequently hanged. God Himself actually drew David's attention to Saul's crimes against the Gibeonites. When David consulted the Lord as to why they were suffering through a three-year long famine, God asserted, "It is for Saul and his bloody house, because he put the Gibeonites to death" (v. 1). It seems that Shimei's beef was also with God. As a side note, even though this account came in a chapter after the story we are currently investigating in 2 Samuel, it most likely occurred earlier in David's reign and was compiled with a few other stories the author wanted to include at the end of the book.[17]

Shimei not only referred to David as a murderer, but also a "worthless fellow" (2 Samuel 16:7). This phrase varies a little in the different versions of the Bible; such as "scoundrel" (NIV), "man of Belial" (KJV), "you rogue" (NKJV), and "worthless man" (ESV). Perhaps Kyle McCarter expresses Shimei's disgust for David the best with his translation—"fiend of hell."[18] Shimei believed that David's current predicament with Absalom's rebellion was divine justice carried out by the Lord due to the "evil" he perpetrated against the house of Saul.

Shimei's tirade was unfounded. His facts were wrong. He was misinformed. His biases errantly skewed his perceptions. He imagined a possible story and believed it was the truth. He risked his life based on a total misunderstanding of the circumstances. And it was actually Saul's house that had the innocent blood of the Gibeonites on it. All the hate and bitterness inside him was for naught.

While in leadership at NASA, I occasionally dealt with conflicts that took place between two or more employees. I still remember how my initial impressions about what happened often proved wrong. After first talking to a reliable source, I sometimes thought I had everything figured out. However, as I continued to investigate the circumstances, others kept filling in details that I did not initially have available to me. I started to realize there were other ways to interpret what happened. Different biases, relationships, worldviews, perceptions, and experiences can easily color one's understanding of any situation. And on rare occasions, I have even come across those who outright lied to me and threw me far afield from the truth with their distorted and untrue "facts." Some people are remarkably good liars and do not hesitate to use their sleazy skill. "Shimeis" are plentiful in our world. Please don't become one! Make sure your understanding of things comes from and across reliable sources. Don't only check your sources, but try to understand their point-of-view, and why they may be shaping a story in a particular way. Do not let the media, friend, relative, or anybody turn you into a hatemonger!

In the not-too-distant past, a friend sent me an inflammatory political email. Guess what? This particular one got me "inflamed." So what did I do? I forwarded it to a select group of friends, and let them know of my disgust for the political shenanigans mentioned in the email. Thankfully, one of my friends replied back and shared some information that proved the original email contained a lot of misinformation. Wow, how easily I was duped! What a sucker! Embarrassed that I had forwarded it to some of my friends, I knew it was time to eat a little crow. Fortunately, I had not sent it to many people, so I took the time to contact each of them and apologize for passing along the inflammatory untruths. I then approached my friend who had sent me the original email and shared with him that it was deceptive and inaccurate. I told him that I was going to be more accountable in the future for anything I forwarded to others and hoped he would do the same. His response was kind of flippant and lackadaisical, as he just shrugged it off and indicated, "Oh well, there is a lot of that kind of stuff out there." It did not bother him; I hope it bothers you. Let's be accountable for what we tell and send to others. And perhaps rather than trying to inflame others, let's help them understand the truth of a matter, so they can make intelligent choices versus emotional ones. Let's not contribute to the creation of one more "Shimei."

The Response

No one directly addressed Shimei. He made untrue, hurtful accusations, but nobody tried to correct him or threw curses his way. Silence in such situations is often the best tactic. David had let the words of a fool provoke him in the past. Nabal's spiteful words sent David into a rage, and it took God's intervention, through the gracious words of Abigail, to stop David from killing all the males associated with the fool's household (see Ch. 1). David learned a valuable lesson from that experience: Never let the words of a raging fool pervert the attitudes of your heart and drive your actions. With Absalom's rebellion, David was immersed in a life and death struggle and was not about to give foolish Shimei any of his attention or consideration. Please note that this story painted Shimei as a wretched individual. He walked parallel to the group at a distance while spewing slanderous speech and throwing rocks and sand. Living in his own make-believe world, Shimei was a lone Benjamite and bitter fool who took aim at the innocent. Yes, he deserved to be ignored.

Abishai responded to Shimei's caustic antics, though not directly to the seething Benjamite, but to David. Abishai must not have learned the same lesson David did about letting a fool provoke you. He assuredly was present during the incident with Nabal, but his warrior ways came to the surface on hearing Shimei cursing the king. In the ancient Hebrew culture, to call someone "a dog" was to disdainfully point out their insignificance. To Abishai, Shimei was not only insignificant, but as a "dead dog," he was doubly so. Cursing your ruler was against the Old Law (Exodus 22:28), and with David's permission, Abishai stood ready to be Shimei's executioner and cut off his head. Violence was not an unusual solution for David's general, as he also asked to kill Saul on another occasion (1 Samuel 26:8). Fortunately for Shimei, David kept his head—as Abishai sought to remove one. David immediately distanced himself from Abishai's barbaric desire, when he expressed in anguish: "What have I to do with you, O sons of Zeruiah?" (v. 10). David made it clear that he did not share in Abishai and Joab's desire to solve many of the problems they faced with violence (Joab was Abishai's brother and related to David through his stepsister).

What came next was absolutely shocking. The sweet psalmist viewed Shimei's cursing through a spiritual lens. David responded to his tormentor, not with more cursing, but with an act of faith.[19] He let Abishai and his traveling companions know that God was at work, and as such, let Shimei rant away. What was meant to be cruel, God could turn into good. What was meant to injure, God could use to heal. Shimei threw stones, David threw himself on the mercy of God.

David reminds us that we have a God who "looks on." God is a Merciful Seer! Let's respond to the spiteful attacks of others by acting humbly and graciously in return. Turn their words, meant to harm, into opportunities to strengthen our faith and rely on God. Others may want to shake your faith, but God can strengthen it.[20] David refused to allow Shimei's thoughtless words to have any undue influence on him. Will you do the same when a Shimei comes your way? One will come your way.

The Rest of the Story

Once Joab treacherously killed Absalom (2 Samuel 18), David was restored as king. His flight from Jerusalem took him east of the Jordan River, so David needed to make the arduous trek back to Jerusalem. As he came to the eastern edge of the Jordan, the people of Judah came to escort their victorious king across the river. Guess who also came with this throng of rejoicing Judahites?

> Then Shimei the son of Gera, the Benjamite who was from Bahurim, hurried and came down with the men of Judah to meet King David. There were a thousand men of Benjamin with him, with Ziba the servant of the house of Saul, and his fifteen sons and his twenty servants with him; and they rushed to the Jordan before the king. Then they kept crossing the ford to bring over the king's household, and to do what was good in his sight. And Shimei the son of Gera fell down before the king as he was about to cross the Jordan. So he said to the king, "Let not my lord consider me guilty, nor remember what your servant did wrong on the day when my lord the king came out from Jerusalem, so that the king would take *it* to heart. For your servant knows that

I have sinned; therefore behold, I have come today, the first of all the house of Joseph to go down to meet my lord the king." But Abishai the son of Zeruiah said, "Should not Shimei be put to death for this, because he cursed the Lord's anointed?" David then said, "What have I to do with you, O sons of Zeruiah, that you should this day be an adversary to me? Should any man be put to death in Israel today? For do I not know that I am king over Israel today?" The king said to Shimei, "You shall not die." Thus the king swore to him (2 Samuel 19:16-23).

When I was a deacon years ago, I used to organize a fellowship activity that we called "Guess Who's Coming to Dinner." People would sign up for whether they wanted to host a meal or be a guest. I then would strategically assign who was going where. I notified the host of the number of guests for whom they should prepare and whether they needed to account for any special considerations, such as allergies and serious dislikes. I would mail the guests a map with a name and address to where they were going. A lot of anticipation was in the air, so when the doorbell rang at 6:00 p.m. that Saturday night, you truly wanted to shout, "Guess Who?"

I could not begin to imagine what ran through David's mind when Shimei suddenly showed up to greet him. It was most certainly a "guess who" moment. Shimei displayed a similar unbridled passion on the king's return, though this time it did not involve any vile speech. Notice how Shimei was portrayed in this scene: He "hurried" to meet David; he did not wait for David to come to Bahurim; he crossed over the Jordan to go to him; before he was alone, now he is with 1,000 Benjamites; previously he stood defiantly cursing the king, now he humbly threw himself on the ground before him; he was the first to make it to David; and the passion that once fueled his cursing, now energized his pleading. Stones were once his shaming missiles, now he humbly groveled amongst them at David's feet. How things in life can so quickly change!

As Shimei admitted his wrongdoing and sought forgiveness from David, Abishai remained true to form. He still wanted to kill the two-faced Benjamite. Abishai's vengeful spirit would not detract David from the reality of the day. He was still "king over Israel." It was time to celebrate, not kill his subjects. Shimei was given a reprieve—for the time being.

On David's deathbed, we learn that Shimei's pardon would be revoked under Solomon's reign.

> Behold, there is with you Shimei the son of Gera the Benjamite, of Bahurim; now it was he who cursed me with a violent curse on the day I went to Mahanaim. But when he came down to me at the Jordan, I swore to him by the Lord, saying, 'I will not put you to death with the sword.' Now therefore, do not let him go unpunished, for you are a wise man; and you will know what you ought to do to him, and you will bring his gray hair down to Sheol with blood" (1 Kings 2:8-9).

Some scholars think that David differed only slightly from the violent sons of Zeruiah. So did he carry to the grave a vengeful spirit concerning Shimei? Perhaps the initial reprieve was politically motivated and part of a larger strategy to keep a firm hold on the kingdom. Even though such speculations have merit, I believe another deeply held attitude motivated David's deathbed sentence against Shimei. David held the "Lord's anointed" in extremely high regard as seen in the stories in 1 Samuel 24 and 26 and 2 Samuel 1. The Torah did not specify the punishment for cursing the king (Exodus 22:28). However, within Abishai's question the common understanding appeared to be that it was a capital offense—"Should not Shimei be put to death for this, *because* he cursed the Lord's anointed?" (2 Samuel 19:21; italics added for emphasis). Shimei himself not only felt that he wronged the king, but that he "sinned" (v. 20) by breaking the law concerning cursing the king. It was a transgression he wanted David to forget and not hold him guilty.

So on his deathbed, David viewed Shimei's cursing as a "violent" (or grievous) act against the Lord's anointed, and as such, required death. David temporarily pardoned him, and it was now up to Solomon to use his wisdom to find a way to carry out the death sentence. As David said to Shimei, "I will not put you to death" (1 Kings 2:9), and he did not. But for this grievous crime against the king, Solomon did.

> Now the king sent and called for Shimei and said to him, "Build for yourself a house in Jerusalem and live there, and do not go out from there to any place. For on the day you go out and cross over the brook Kidron, you will know for certain that you shall surely die; your blood shall be on your own head." Shimei then said to the king, "The word is good. As my lord the king has said, so your servant will do." So Shimei lived in Jerusalem many days.
>
> But it came about at the end of three years, that two of the servants of Shimei ran away to Achish son of Maacah, king of Gath. And they told Shimei, saying, "Behold, your servants are in Gath." Then Shimei arose and saddled his donkey, and went to Gath to Achish to look for his servants. And Shimei went and brought his servants from Gath. It was told Solomon that Shimei had gone from Jerusalem to Gath, and had returned. So the king sent and called for Shimei and said to him, "Did I not make you swear by the Lord and solemnly warn you, saying, 'You will know for certain that on the day you depart and go anywhere, you shall surely die'? And you said to me, 'The word which I have heard is good.' Why then have you not kept the oath of the Lord, and the command which I have laid on you?" The king also said to Shimei, "You know all the evil which you acknowledge in your heart, which you did to my father David; therefore the Lord shall return your evil on your own head. But King Solomon shall be blessed, and the throne of David shall be established before the Lord forever." So the king commanded Benaiah the son of Jehoiada, and he went out and fell upon him so that he died. Thus the kingdom was established in the hands of Solomon (1 Kings 2:36-46).

Shimei broke the Torah by cursing the king then violated an oath made directly with Solomon. Before Solomon had him put to death, the king reminded him of the "evil" he carried out against the Lord's anointed. His mouth got him into trouble, and he thought his shrewd words had gotten him out of it. *If only* he could have controlled that tongue in the beginning. Surely, with deep remorse, you have cried out, "If only I had not said...!" Words from bitter and enraged hearts cut deep. Control them, and eliminate "if only" from your vocabulary.

Parting Thoughts

Today, Christians are under attack in the U.S. like never before in my lifetime. The media often portrays us as intolerant and mean-spirited to others. Since our norms are often counter-cultural, they tend to marginalize our views, saying we "are behind the times." The entertainment industry has also joined the anti-Christian onslaught, though in more subtle ways. Have you ever noticed that "religious" roles in many of today's movies are negatively depicted? They often paint a distasteful picture of this character by making them out to be judgmental, hypocritical, non-intellectual, and even true goofballs. We probably could come up with many reasons for this, but one deals directly with our speech.

About a decade ago, the Barna Research Group released some research that revealed that Christians are largely perceived as hypocritical and judgmental (among other things) by non-Christians between the ages of 16 to 29.[21] We could say, "Well, that's just their perception." Personally, I would prefer to be perceived as loving, serving, and trustworthy. So how did they form such an opinion? The media and entertainment industry surely contribute to some degree. But in large part, maybe we are directly responsible for such views. I have asked a number of ministers about Barna's findings, and not one has said that we do not bear the brunt of the responsibility.

When my daughter worked as a waitress in her college years, she once told me that Christians were sometimes hard to deal with as they flocked into the restaurants after Sunday morning services were over. My wife and I can independently attest to this troubling opinion that my daughter expressed. On one occasion, we joined another couple for lunch at a local restaurant after church let out on Sunday morning. During our time there, we started joking around with our waiter. We conspicuously bore the brand of "church-goers" due to our dress, and he made some reference to it. After the conclusion of the meal, he told us that he really appreciated our friendliness and lightheartedness and enjoyed serving us. He then shockingly added that most of the wait staff does not like working Sundays because of how they are treated by Christians. Whoa, that was disturbing! On another occasion, my wife and I were eating breakfast with a Christian relative at a popular chain restaurant, and things were fine until there was a problem with his coupon. He then verbally bullied this poor waitress to the point that I felt like curling up in a ball in the corner of our booth. It was nothing short of embarrassing and shameful! On listening to a talk-show segment on a local Christian radio station, the host presented the same type of information, further validating my own experiences. I know you can come up with a lot of good examples to counter my bad ones, but I am convinced this is a much larger problem than we would like to admit.

I have listened to similar complaints through the years from those in the medical field as well. I remember one story concerning a young girl who had just started working in a particular medical office. The scheduler had to go home a little early one day during the new girl's first week, so when the phone rang, she dutifully answered it. On the other end of the phone was a man who desired to schedule an appointment for his wife. The new girl tried to handle all his questions, but did not know all the ins-

and-outs of the office yet and could not give him all the answers he sought. After hanging up, the man hurried down to this office in a huff. He wanted to see what kind of place it was that could not handle his questions. When he arrived, he lit into this poor girl unmercifully, to the point she started crying. He was so out-of-line that some of the patients that witnessed the incident were ready to come to her aid and get into a fight with the obnoxious man. He finally relented when he understood the situation and the sweet nature of this young girl, but the deed was done. So what did he do next? He brought some Christian brochures for others to read, when he brought his wife for her appointment.

So what is my point? "We have a problem, Houston," and we need to address it in our churches if we want to have any credibility in reaching a lost world. We may profess love and concern, but our words and actions often demonstrate otherwise.

Jesus said the following,

> But the things that proceed out of the mouth from the heart, and those defile the man. For out of the heart come evil thoughts, murders, adulteries, fornications, thefts, false witness, slanders. These are the things which defile the man; but to eat with unwashed hands does not defile the man" (Matthew 15:18-20).

So what kind of speech is your heart producing? If our hearts are formed in the trait of compassion, we will speak caring words to others. If in kindness, we will address people in considerate ways. If in gentleness, our speech will take on a tender tone. You may say, "Well, I am just a frank person." "I just tell it like it is." Well, maybe you need to go to the school of the fruit of the Spirit. Of course we need to be assertive with others in some situations, but assertiveness does not equal aggressiveness. In our frankness or assertiveness, we can be gentle, kind, and loving. Frank speech frequently has selfish origins. It is how "you" want to say things, not taking into account what others actually need to hear and how they need to hear it. A friend recently asked me to review something he had written. The writing style unfortunately had some fatal flaws. So I asked him if I could speak to him frankly about the material. After he said *yes*, I was as gentle as possible in explaining the flaws with his work of passion, but made sure he thoroughly understood what he needed to address.

"Telling it like it is" speech is often fraught with judgmentalism. It exudes self-righteousness. You have it all figured out, and they don't. It's a "My way or the highway" type of mentality. Even if you have it all figured out, exude patience with others, promoting peace with words that facilitate healing and maturing. Remember, Paul said it is those who possess a "spirit of gentleness" that are to help restore those overtaken by sin (Galatians 6:1). God wants them restored, not shamed and punished. Let's partner with God's Spirit to expose our un-Christian traits and facilitate the maturation of the fruit of the Spirit.

When encountering problems with products or services, I always try to treat the customer service representatives graciously. And by using this approach, they often go the extra mile, in return, to solve the issue. Yes, there are those rare incidents when someone reacts rudely, but we don't need to respond by throwing verbal stones and bullying them to get our way. If you treat people graciously, you're likely to be treated that way in return.

Please, don't treat others in loving ways to change their perceptions nor to be treated in a particular manner. Treat them that way because you care about them. Be Christian! God so loves us, so let us love others.

Questions

1. What was wrong with Shimei's outburst against David? To what was Shimei potentially referring when he said that David was guilty of the "bloodshed of the house of Saul?" Was his assessment accurate?

2. How did David handle Shimei's cursing on the road as he was fleeing Jerusalem? How would you have handled such an incident? What specifically can we learn from David in this situation?

3. Have you ever jumped to a conclusion about a particular situation that you later learned was incorrect? What could you have done differently to judge the situation in a better way?

4. David asked Solomon to execute Shimei for his "grievous" cursing incident? Why do you believe he did this? Was it justified?

5. The Barna Group found from surveying non-Christians in the age range of 16 to 29 that many Christians are perceived as hypocritical and judgmental. Do you believe these results? Why or why not? How do the things we say impact this perception?

6. Explain how frank speech can be a problem and how we might improve on it? How might this problem be exasperated on social media? How can we personally guard against it?

CHAPTER 4

Hophni and Phineas
Preying Priests

Keep deception and lies far from me,
give me neither poverty nor riches;
Feed me with the food that is my portion,
That I not be full and deny You and say, "Who is the Lord?"
Or that I not be in want and steal,
And profane the name of my God.

(Proverbs 30:8-9)

W hen my wife and I were quite a bit younger, we worked with the youth at our local congregation. We hosted devotions, took them on camping trips, and organized various fellowship activities. During this time, a kindhearted teenage boy started coming to our church and began attending the youth activities. He had a quiet demeanor and a sweet personality. I typically don't refer to other males as "sweet," but no other word properly describes this young man's spirit. His smile put a smile on my face. I loved joking around with him just to see that radiant, infectious smile. Since he was a high school senior when he joined our youth group, it was not long before he started attending a local community college. He stopped participating in the youth program at that time but still came regularly to most of the other activities at our church.

My relationship with this friendly young man continued to grow, and I felt like I needed to help bring him to a saving faith in Jesus. So when the moment seemed right, I asked if I could study the Bible with him. With no hesitancy, he responded, "Yes." Elated over his acceptance, we immediately set up a convenient time for him to come over to our home. With his exposure to many sermons, classes, and devotionals at our church over a couple of years, I made some assumptions concerning his spiritual leanings and chose some key passages to kick off our study. When we met for the first time, we read the passages together, and I asked him a question or two. Sometimes I wanted him to comment on the meaning of what we had read, and I also attempted to bring about a little introspection. His responses to some of my questions left me a bit perplexed. I remember asking myself, *Did I make a mistake in my assessment of his spirituality?* I stopped and looked him in the eyes and asked, "Do you believe in God?" He said, "No, I am an atheist." Shocked and bewildered, I immediately responded, "Why have you been coming all this time?" He flashed one of those warm-hearted smiles at me and said, "I like the people. People of this moral caliber and ethics are who I want to hang around."

Motivations vary as to why some individuals attend church and serve in various capacities. Obviously, I possess no powers to look into human hearts to determine their motivations, though some have shared them with me both directly and indirectly. Such insights have not only been surprising at times, but also quite revealing as to the source of some behaviors. What drives our attendance and service may often be spiritually healthy, but there are times that it can be unhealthy. A biblical example may help spur our thinking on this subject.

Trouble in Shiloh

First Samuel's author opened his book with the heartwarming story of the birth of Samuel. Hannah, Samuel's mother, desperately pleaded with God for a son, and in return she vowed, "I will give him to the Lord all the days of his life, and a razor shall never come on his head" (1 Samuel 1:11). God granted her request, and she gave birth to Samuel. After she weaned him, Hannah took the infant to Eli, the high priest, at Shiloh to serve God. The tabernacle, along with the Ark of the Covenant, was located there at this point in time, so she knew that young Samuel would learn the ways of the priesthood from Eli as worshipers went to this special city to sacrifice to the Lord.

After the author gave us Hannah's beautiful song of praise and thanksgiving to the Lord, he immediately shifted gears and recorded a disturbing story about Eli's sons.

> Now the sons of Eli were worthless men; they did not know the Lord and the custom of the priests with the people. When any man was offering a sacrifice, the priest's servant would come while the meat was boiling, with a three-pronged fork in his hand. Then he would thrust it into the pan, or kettle, or caldron, or pot; all that the fork brought up the priest would take for himself. Thus they did in Shiloh to all the Israelites who came there. Also, before they burned the fat, the priest's servant would come and say to the man who was sacrificing, "Give the priest meat for roasting, as he will not take boiled meat from you, only raw." If the man said to him, "They must surely burn the fat first, and then take as much as you desire," then he would say, "No, but you shall give *it to me* now; and if not, I will take it by force." Thus the sin of the young men was very great before the Lord, for the men despised the offering of the Lord (1 Samuel 2:12-17).

Ouch!!! What a horrible epithet for Eli's sons, and *terrifying* only begins to describe the concluding remark. "Great" in its own monumental nature was not adequate enough to properly depict their sin before the Lord; the immensity and egregiousness of it required the description "very great." In most movies and books today, such a portrayal would not bode well for such characters in the scenes to come. Perhaps ancient Hebrew storytellers knew such techniques as well.

Hophni and Phinehas were first introduced in 1 Samuel 1 as "priests to the Lord" at Shiloh (v.3). Yet in the passage under investigation, the author seemed to disparagingly omit their names. He also appeared to incorporate a play on words right out of the chute. Immediately after referring to them as the "sons of Eli," they were then designated as "sons of belial." In other words, these two were not priestly; they were lawless and worthless. Per Unger, *belial* in the Old Testament should not be taken as a proper name, and the expression "son of belial" was a Semitic idiom for a "worthless" or "lawless" man.[22]

Another extremely troubling remark defined their worthlessness: "They did not know the Lord." We will discuss this in more detail in a moment, but let's first look at the evidence provided for such a statement in the two examples given. First, when God's people came to Shiloh to make a peace offering to the Lord, the priests misappropriated some of the worshipers' meat, which was designated for an ensuing sacred family feast (vv. 13-14). Not satisfied with their portion defined by the Mosaic Law (Leviticus 7:28-36), the two young priests had their servants thrust an assumedly large three-pronged fork into the pot where the worshipers' meat was boiling. Whatever amount and type of meat was wrestled from the pot, these thieving "priests" kept for themselves. To make matters worse, this was not some occasional or haphazard incident. These priests instituted this gluttonous and greedy practice as the norm at Shiloh.

The second example that described the priest's worthlessness showed their blatant disregard for God (vv.15-16). Not only did they help themselves to the worshipers' portion of the sacrificial meat, they took from God as well. In other words, they basically robbed God.[23] More pious and virtuous than the priests and their servants, a worshiper reminded them of their priestly duty by making the plea, "Please take of my part of the offering, just first burn the fat of my sacrifice to God as described in the Law" (my words). Taken back by the worshiper's comment, the priest's servant resulted to bullying tactics. What started out as a request, turned into a demand that would be backed up with violence. So yes, the sons of Eli were "worthless," "did not know God" and their sin was "very great before the Lord!"

As is often the case with sin, there are unintended consequences involving others. In the case of Hophni and Phinehas, though, I am sure they could not have cared less. The author concluded the story with this statement, "for the men despised the offering of the Lord" (v. 17). This can be interpreted in two different ways. The question involves who were "the men." One possible interpretation is that "the men" are Hophni and Phinehas and their associated servants. Certainly, by their actions, they despised or held in contempt the offering of the Lord. Another interpretation suggests that "the men" were the men of Israel. I believe this is the preferred rendering. Throughout this passage the author used a separate word in the Hebrew (translated as "man" and "men") to distinguish the worshipers from the "priest's servant" and "young men." In verse 17, the term takes on the plural form, and thus included all the male worshipers who came to Shiloh.

Personally, I have never witnessed an act by an individual that caused church members to "despise" all or some portion of our worship. Part of the "despising" of the offering though, surely involved avoiding it altogether in the future because of the priests and their servants' conduct. Would you want to go to worship knowing you would be subjected to bullying and taken advantage of, while God's commandments were willfully ignored? Probably not. Some behaviors by our brothers and sisters may also cause us to avoid going to worship. I am not saying that is the appropriate response, but many people are conflict-adverse and would prefer not to deal with others who are exhibiting poor or questionable behavior. You may say, "No way I am going to let another's behavior drive what I do!" But I think most of us have used an avoidance tactic or two at some juncture in our lives.

At one point during my career, I was in a fairly small staff office. I was extremely busy with a lot of irons in the fire. Our boss was well liked, but had a horrible habit of constantly volunteering our office to take on "low value" action items. We were not staffed for such activities, and this extra work was a legitimate burden. Of course, she looked good by volunteering, but we suffered for her self-centered motivations. If she was ever coming from some executive meeting, and you met up with her in the hallway, expect to be the "stuckee" with some unwanted assignment. To this day, I can still visualize a particular circumstance involving her. I had a lot of urgent activities on my plate, and I hurried out of my office to take care of a particular situation. In the distance, I saw my boss slowly making her way toward me down a long hallway. Yep, she had just come from one of those executive meetings. My internal collision avoidance software placed me on red alert. A debris field of unwanted work was heading straight for me. Knowing that I could not afford to take on any new tasks, I ducked into a nearby stairwell and went down one flight of stairs. I then made my way along the hallway below my boss in the same direction as I was previously heading. After going a safe distance, I went back up the stairs on the other side of where I had initially seen her. Relieved, I scurried off to take care of the pressing matter I needed to handle. Personally, I am not proud of that story, as such a course of action was not one of my typical behaviors. Nonetheless, her actions resulted in my desire to *avoid* her on that given day.

So what kind of behaviors at church might result in someone's avoiding going to church altogether or skipping out on certain activities. You can make your own list, but let me stimulate your thinking with a few examples. Before we start, I need to make one thing clear: You are responsible for your behaviors and no one else's. They may make poor choices, but let's try to not contribute to those choices in negative ways. To start, politics is typically not a good topic of conversation when we gather together. Political ideologies can vary greatly across a congregation. Regrettably, many folks feel strongly about their positions and can easily make disparaging remarks about people who don't agree with them—lumping them into such categories as "ignorant," "anti-American," or the like. Obviously, such comments can be personally offensive. Rather than defending themselves, some people may choose to avoid the conflict and either stay home or switch churches. I remember one man whose subtle comments made me realize he viewed armed conflicts a little differently than others. In fact, one church member's comment on a social media site lumped people like him in the "category" of "not loving America." In actuality, this man was a pacifist and had good biblical reasons for his views about the subject. Most certainly, whether I agreed with him or not, I respected his position and held him in high regard.

"Policing" behavior is another activity many desire to shun. I have never seen a badge for the "gospel police," but some have decided to take on such a role. Of course, we need to follow sound doctrine, but many things fall in the realm of opinion. When someone constantly nitpicks at every little thing others say, something is amiss. At its core, such a practice is frequently egocentric and can fall into the realm of judgmentalism. Often, these "policemen" want to show their superiority with Scripture, unlovingly squashing thoughtful views of others. Typically, it comes down to, "I am right and you are wrong!" "No need to discuss the matter further." Unfortunately, these people attract others who share their opinion and run off well-intentioned Christians who do not. As Paul stated, "Knowledge makes arrogant, but love edifies" (1 Corinthians 8:1). Paul was not against pursuing knowledge, but he would be against using it as a weapon to divide a body of Christians and belittle fellow believers. Living a life of love in concert with truth is our goal. Jesus was the perfect embodiment of "grace and truth" (ref. John 1:14). Let's address the views and opinions of others with respect and in loving ways. And yes, doctrinal error can be addressed in gracious ways, as well.

A Bible class that is regularly commandeered by one of its students can become a source of frustration for many people. For me, I just love talking about God's Word and classes offer a wonderful venue to participate in that. Nevertheless, I must be ever vigilant not to overdo it. I've seen times when a well-meaning individual gave a long discourse on their position on a particular topic, jumping from one bible passage to another. Or they shared a story that went on and on and on. And on!!! When we behave like this on a routine basis, we may want to consider cutting back on our comments. Let the teacher have an opportunity to teach and share what they prepared. Also, value what others have to say by giving them time to say it. Allowing our fellow class-members the opportunity to share their views or personal life experiences may facilitate what needs to be taught on a specific subject. Arrogance is a trait that can cause us to monopolize a class. We might think, *My opinion matters more than others. I have a better grasp on this subject than everybody else does. Everyone else wants to know what I think on this matter.* Maybe some do, but we need to lose the attitude. Remember, God can be at work in our classes, and it's not only through what you have to say.

There's one last behavior on my list to share with you. We could probably talk about a number of different sins that may cause people to avoid coming to our churches and/or its activities. However, this particular one overcomes a large number of otherwise devout Christians. Many church-goers participate, tolerate, and even accept this practice. It rears its ugly head in private conversations and in groups. Neither men nor women are immune to its enticing ways. Have you guessed what it is? I am referring to gossip. Many people believe this sin is mostly associated with women. Think again! Men fall into its clutches just as easily. I remember one man who stopped attending a men's prayer breakfast because of all the gossiping that took place. He eventually left that church altogether. When his new congregation wanted to start a men's prayer breakfast, he fought against it because of his previous distasteful experiences. Obviously, nothing is wrong with having a men's prayer breakfast; in fact, my experiences have been rather positive, but when the gossip train starts rolling, many tend to jump on board. Sometimes we get a little confused about what gossiping actually is. I remember one nice Christian woman who was challenged by a person close to her regarding gossiping about a particular person. She said, "It's not gossip; it's true." Gossiping may persist of lies, slander, and distorted facts, or it may simply involve the truth. And that truth may be extraordinarily hurtful to others. Typically, the best course of action is to avoid talking negatively about others altogether and revealing confidential information. If others start going in those directions, you need to change the course of the conversation or plainly say that you do not want to talk about such things. People who are recovering from a sinful past need healing, not the added shame that malicious gossip can bring their way. Gossip is not loving speech. Let's love with our speech and our actions. No one will want to avoid that.vw

The Trouble Grows

Fortunately, the author gives us a peek into Samuel's positive development after the discouraging story about the sons of Eli. Samuel was noted as "ministering" and growing "before the Lord." But Eli's sons were not reined in, and the trouble at Shiloh continued to grow. Eli finally tried to address the worsening situation but would his warnings be heeded? No!

> Now Eli was very old; and he heard all that his sons were doing to all Israel, and how they lay with the women who served at the doorway of the tent of meeting. He said to them, "Why do you do such things, the evil things that I hear from all these people? No, my sons; for the report is not good which I hear the LORD's people circulating. If one man sins against another, God will mediate for him; but if a man sins against the LORD,

who can intercede for him?" But they would not listen to the voice of their father, for the LORD desired to put them to death (1 Samuel 2:22-25).

Not only were Hophni and Phinehas debasing the priestly service involving the offerings, but they continued to abuse their office by enticing the "women who served" at the Tabernacle to have sexual relations with them. These women came to serve the Lord, while the two perverted sons of Eli served themselves to these women. Instead of honoring them as holy, they degraded them like pagan temple prostitutes.

Eli gave his two sons a dire warning. As judge of Israel at the time, Eli informed them that God could mediate for them if they had sinned against another individual, but they sinned against God. No mediation awaited them, only divine judgment. Surely, Eli hoped his sons would repent and throw themselves at the feet of a merciful God, but it was too late for those two. Judgment had already taken place. Eli's pleas fell on deaf ears; in this case, it wasn't because of the obstinate attitudes of his sons, but because the Lord intervened—"for the Lord desired to put them to death." Wow, that is one scary verse! Our modern sensibilities desire a God of grace, which He is, but we must remember, justice is one of the core characteristics of God. Hophni and Phinehas's hearts had long ago been hardened by the constancy of their evil. God took no pleasure in sentencing them to death, but he was pleased to bring back order amongst His people and avert the corruption that ensued at the hands of these evil priests.[24]

With such a tragic outcome, it's hard not to ask, "What happened in this household? How was it possible for Hophni and Phinehas to turn into such hellions? Were they not brought up in the ways of the Lord? Did they not witness their father serving God in the tabernacle and righteously judging the issues of the day in Israel? What happened!?!" Unfortunately, we are not given a direct answer, only some cursory information to put together a possible scenario. My thoughts lie in how Eli was depicted. Basically, he appeared in this story as a bad father and high priest. He seemed either to ignore, tolerate, or be totally oblivious to the travesty involving the offerings. No correcting of his sons was recorded until he heard of their sinful activities "from all these people." At this point, God had already judged them. Why did he not rebuke his sons on hearing the first incident? He only goes to them at a "very old" age, probably way too late to have an impact on their lives. Through a prophetic messenger of God and a vision from God Himself, the Lord directly indicted Eli.

> Why do you kick at My sacrifice and at My offering which I have commanded *in My* dwelling, and honor your sons above Me, by making yourselves fat with the choicest of every offering of My people Israel (1 Samuel 2:29)?

> For I have told him that I am about to judge his house forever for the iniquity which he knew, because his sons brought a curse on themselves and he did not rebuke them (1 Samuel 3:13).

By not stopping Hophni and Phinehas's abuses as priests, Eli honored his sons over God. As high priest, he was ultimately accountable for what took place concerning the offerings. As a father, he should have been more aware at an earlier stage of his sons' evil antics and disciplined them appropriately. God directly indicted Eli along with his sons. These pilfering priests may have stolen some of the people's portions of the offering, but Eli, along with his sons, became fat from feasting on these "choicest" cuts of meat. He did not rebuke them "for the iniquity which he knew." Surely, a life of overlooking his sons' wicked ways came back to haunt this distraught father, as God's judgment against Eli's house shortly came about.

Again, we might still ask, "Why did those boys turn out so bad?" This side of heaven, we will not know for certain, but perhaps Eli's duties as judge and high priest caused him to be away from home too often during his sons' formative years. I know from personal experience how easily we can become consumed with a job that we truly love and to which we are extremely devoted. Around the midpoint of my career with NASA, I started working on the International Space Station (ISS) Program. With the ISS behind schedule and over-budget, some of our senior managers decided to deploy a number of our top engineers and resource planners into the contractors' manufacturing facilities. Their task was to root out the issues that kept us from making meaningful progress. Any problem that we could not quickly solve, we were to bring to management's attention, so that we could place the required resources on it to bring about a speedy resolution. We were also chartered to assure the test program for each ISS major element was sound. And in conjunction with that, we needed to develop a way to connect as many of these elements together at one time to test them in an integrated fashion before launching them individually on the Space Shuttle. I was put in charge of overseeing these test activities.

This formidable assignment was exhausting and robbing me of precious family time. The hours were long, and I flew around the country from one contractor facility to another to attend meetings and reviews. Since I was often gone all week, home maintenance, lawn work, bills, and other household responsibilities got pushed into the weekend. Typical family outings on Saturday and Sunday were often displaced by these necessary weekend tasks. On top of that, the job stress and constant traveling with the time zone changes wore me to a frazzle. As you might imagine, the quality of our family life severely suffered during this timeframe.

A lot of the childrearing activities fell on my wife's shoulders. My parenting approach became more reactionary as I learned what my children had done while I was gone. For example, I remember one weekend when I had a serious talk with our children about taking care of our furniture. My wife said she had caught them turning our couch into a trampoline. Because of my stern tone and words, they undoubtedly understood that there would be severe consequences if they did not change their behavior. What happened the following week would forever change my life.

The ensuing Monday after the "couch jumping" conversation, I was supposed to be gone to California the entire week. Good fortune came my way though, as the meeting I attended finished early, so I caught a red-eye flight back to Florida on Thursday night. When my son came in from school on Friday afternoon, he did not realize that I had come home early. Tucked away in the corner of our main living area, I took advantage of the extra time to make an overdue home repair. Unnoticed, I sat and watched my 10-year-old son come loping through this room. He swerved slightly to go around our couch and then headed into the hallway to go to his room. Following closely behind him was one of his friends. He did not take the same path as my son. When he came to our couch, he jumped on it with both feet and placed his hands on the top of the backrest and vaulted himself over the top of it. My son obviously saw his buddy's gymnastic move from the hallway, because he stopped him dead in his tracks. I then overheard my son mildly chastising him, "We do not do that in our home, so please don't jump on our furniture anymore." His friend nonchalantly said, "Ok, no problem," and off they went into my son's bedroom. Sitting there in utter astonishment and pride, my heart, like the Grinch's, must have grown "three sizes that day."

After a moment or two, I called out to my son and said, "Jeremy, please come here." Not knowing I was home, he probably thought that I had seen his friend jump on the couch, and now he was going to "get it." He immediately came back into our main living area and found me standing in the corner. Once he made his way over to me, he looked at me with quizzical and worrisome eyes, and I said to him: "I saw what just happened, and I am very proud of you. I appreciate that you took to heart what we told you about taking care of our furniture. Now go have fun and play with your friend." As I reached out for a quick hug, a tender grin spread across his face that illumined my heart. I realized that my interaction with my children over the previous couple of years had been through negative reinforcement. When I came home from a trip, I learned what they did wrong and tried to be a "good" father and address it. But at the moment that I hugged my son, a revelation came on me like at no time in my past. By witnessing the little things that my children were doing, I could use positive reinforcement as a teaching tool to help reinforce their good behavior. As a tear ran down my face, this dad knew he needed a shift in his priorities.

Right after this incident, I was presented with a wonderful job opportunity that would allow me to stay home a lot more. It took me off a career track that was more lucrative and prestigious, but my family needed a father and husband, not a NASA manager. Therefore, I jumped at the job and never, ever regretted that decision. With more spare time, I started volunteering in various capacities at my children's events, such as chaperoning their church activities, announcing at my daughter's soccer games, raking the jumping pits at my son's track meets, teaching their Bible classes, and helping raise money for their teams' needs. Such involvement allowed me not only to be around my children more, but definitely provided some precious teachable moments. I also could observe their behavior and saw the kids with whom they liked to hang out. But what really amazed me was the depth that was added to our conversations because of my increased involvement in their lives. Not that I was perfect by any means, but my children could watch how a Christian dad handled several situations over the years that followed, since I chose them over pursuing money and prestige. Most certainly, changing jobs was one of the best decisions I ever made.

I shared this long story, because I believe Hophni and Phinehas were deprived of the father they so desperately needed. He just was not there for them. He needed to delegate some responsibilities and spend more time with those boys. When we decide to have children, we take on a remarkable and demanding ministry. One that does not come with a "dad manual," but so many good examples exist in our churches, we need to tap some of that expertise to help us along the way. Be there, Be There, BE THERE for your children, and love on them every step of the way. Some discipline will be required now and then, but they will want to please you. And above all, you need to mature as a Christian, and let them see a godly example in all that you do. It's pretty daunting, but it's so rewarding.

Trouble Alleviated, Hope on the Horizon

Through a prophet and a vision from God to Samuel, Eli learned his two sons had a death sentence hanging over their heads, and the priesthood would be taken from his house. When Israel went to war with the Philistines, Hophni and Phinehas accompanied the Ark of the Covenant to the Israelites' staging area for the war. During the subsequent battle, Israel was severely defeated. Ironically, the evil priests were slain at the hands of an evil enemy. But another tragedy befell Israel that day, the precious and sacred Ark of the Covenant was taken by the pagan Philistines. A Benjamite escaped the slaughter and ran back to Shiloh to tell of the disastrous news. This fortunate survivor shared the following report with Eli.

...."Israel has fled before the Philistines and there has also been a great slaughter among the people, and your two sons also, Hophni and Phinehas, are dead, and the ark of God has been taken." When he mentioned the ark of God, Eli fell off the seat backward beside the gate, and his neck was broken and he died, for he was old and heavy. Thus he judged Israel forty years (1 Samuel 4:17-18).

As Eli became "heavy" from eating the "choicest" portions of Israel's offerings, irony was again at work, because his unchecked indulgences contributed to snapping the neck of the aged priest. A sad, sad legacy.

Everything appeared bleak for Israel, but our wise God was busily at work preparing a new champion for His people.

> Thus Samuel grew and the Lord was with him and let none of his words fail. All Israel from Dan even to Beersheba knew that Samuel was confirmed as a prophet of the Lord. And the Lord appeared again at Shiloh, because the Lord revealed Himself to Samuel at Shiloh by the word of the Lord (1 Samuel 3:19-21).

We should remember that God worked through Eli to train and raise up perhaps Israel's most revered priest, prophet, and judge. Eli had some serious flaws but was not inherently evil like his sons. Is it not amazing how God can work through His people at times? He has a habit and ability of working through us flawed humans for good. God, please open our hearts to always allow You to work through us...may Your goodness reign.

Parting Thoughts

Let's now go back to the disturbing statement that the sons of Eli "did not know the Lord." It is hard to fathom how these two men could serve God in such a capacity, yet not have any regard for Him. Somewhere along the line, they devised a scheme to profit from God's people. Perhaps a friend or servant suggested such an arrangement to them, or maybe they formulated the ill-fated concept themselves. Rather than *preying on* God's people, they should have been *praying for* them. Worshiping and serving God, for some reason, did not produce an experiential relationship with their loving Creator. Their motivations for performing the priestly service became twisted at some point along the way. Can such a thing happen to us? Maybe a good question to ask ourselves is, *Why do we go to church?* There are obviously many reasons that we could give, but let's explore a few to help us evaluate how our motivations might undermine developing a sound relationship with God.

We may be prone to say, "Surely no one today shares the problems of Hophni and Phinehas!" Hopefully not, at least in regard to the evilness of their hearts, but I have seen people try to profit from fellow Christians at church. First, let me briefly mention that I prefer to buy services and products from my brothers and sisters when appropriate and practical. I want to help them out, if possible. But when someone makes us targets at church for their business interests, we have a problem. I remember one individual who wanted my wife and me to participate in a pyramid scheme that he was pushing. As I recall, the man became quite annoyed with us because we chose to not take part. It's acceptable to make our brothers and sisters aware of what we do for a living, but then let them approach us about buying any of our services or products. Let it occur naturally, not by design. When we come to church, our motives should be to profit spiritually, not monetarily.

Many people's primary reason for attending church is for their children's development. They want them to learn about Jesus, mature around other wholesome children, and eventually, develop a saving faith. And of course this is important, but is it of "primary" importance? I would suggest that it is not. Our children need Christian parents who are formed in the image of Christ. They need to see their father and mother relying on Christian principles to deal with life's troubles. They should observe the fruit of the Spirit lavishly pouring forth from their parents. When others are in urgent need, they note that their mom and dad step up to help out. Church attendance should facilitate such maturing and properly equip us to bring the goodness of God into the lives of others. For example, when an airliner loses cabin pressure, the oxygen masks automatically fall from the compartment above your seat. You should don your own mask first, then your child's. If you don't, oxygen deprivation may cause you both to lose your lives as you fumble around with the mask. Spiritually speaking, save your life first, so you can truly help save your child's.

Like in the story of the young man that opened this chapter, you may enjoy good Christian fellowship. I know that I do, but again, is it the "primary" reason for coming to church? Our social circle at church can become our god and control our desire to attend. The social environment becomes the attraction, not God. Your involvement is to develop relationships with others, not God. I would suggest that you attend church to develop a proper relationship with God, and let that aid you in developing healthy Christian relationships with others. If you truly love God, you will love others. Christian fellowship is critical to our development, but not the main reason we should attend.

Some folks love certain aspects of our worship services. They attend because the singing is inspirational or the preacher's sermons are interesting and moving. Expressing ourselves in song to God during worship should be important to us. Likewise, listening to sermons serves to bring about faith and should play a key role in our development. But neither of these worship components should serve as the "primary" reason we come to our church services. Worship should be joyful and inspirational. Nevertheless, our motivation for attending our services is not for participation in a particular aspect of worship. If so, we can easily make it all about us.

But how should we answer the question, "Why do we come to church?" I believe the answer is multi-faceted. First, we should attend because we love God and are forever grateful for what He has done for us in Christ Jesus. Second, we want to truly, deep-down *know* Him and become like Him. Third, because of who He is, we want to seek and encounter Him and respond in worshipful ways. We should yearn to praise God like the seraphim in Isaiah's throne room vision. In experiencing the Lord, these remarkable creatures cannot help but sing out: "Holy, Holy, Holy, is the Lord of hosts, the whole earth is full of His glory" (Isaiah 6:3). Lastly, it's a tool that God designed to equip His people and "to stimulate one another to love and good deeds" (Hebrews 10:24). Attending church, and its various activities, helps us develop a proper relationship with God. I am not so naïve to suggest that coming to "know" God only happens through participating in our church activities. It occurs throughout life and in many facets of our personal Christian walks. Nevertheless, attending church is a key component in bringing about a healthy relationship with our God. God's Spirit dwells there. His people gather there. We are part of the body. Let's not forsake it.

Questions

1. How did the author of 1 Samuel describe Hophni and Phinehas?

2. Have you ever witnessed any behaviors at your church that bothered you? How did you react?

3. What types of behaviors do you believe might cause others to leave your congregation or avoid participating in some capacity? Explain.

4. Explore some possibilities about why Hophni and Phinehas turned out the way they did. What do you think is the most likely?

5. Discuss why positive reinforcement is a superior developmental tool for a parent versus negative reinforcement. What helps facilitate our using positive reinforcement?

6. What is the "primary" reason(s) that *you* attend church? Discuss why you believe this to be the case.

7. How can some of the good aspects of church life become spiritually unhealthy if we make them our "primary" reasons for attending church?

CHAPTER 5

Doeg
The Opportunist

Will they not go astray who devise evil?
But kindness and truth will be to those who devise good.

(Proverbs 14:22)

High school sports set this man on an exciting trajectory. Now in his senior years, he wanted to give back by helping young men develop in the sport of his first love. As a former collegiate all-American and professional of the Canadian Football League, he had a lot of experience and knowledge to share, so he took a head football coaching job at a small-town high school. With his coaching staff in place, he was ready to start the arduous task of instilling a strong team ethic and winning ways in his young men. Though behind the scenes, someone set out to undermine his leadership, despite his decorated athletic past and unselfish motivation.

With practices barely underway, one of the assistant coaches became desirous of the head coaching position. In his youthful zeal, he felt superior to his senior boss and thought he could relate better to the players. He mistakenly took the head coach's slow-paced and methodical decision-making as senility. Even though the head coach's mental prowess had naturally declined some because of age, he still had the focus, fortitude, and competency to lead this team. Nevertheless, the envious assistant turned stealthily subversive. He initially started bad-mouthing the head coach in front of some of the players. He then progressed to distorting the circumstances surrounding some of the head coach's decisions to convince some of the key players that the ex-pro was senile and encouraged them to complain about the older man to their parents. This pigskin rebel also started to privately voice his misleading concerns with the other coaches in an attempt to sway them to his way of thinking. No opportunity slipped past this weasel to belittle the old football coach before parents and school administrators. Rather than coaching young men to winning ways, he coached up others to do his malicious bidding. Nothing seemed too low for this dissident assistant, as he even stooped to calling some plays during the games, which resulted in disastrous consequences, hoping they would reflect poorly on the head coach.

Before long, the principal had a full-blown mutiny on his hand. He still held this football star of the past in high regard, but was backed into a corner. He decided to let the head coach go and replaced him with the treasonous assistant before the season was over. You probably have witnessed such situations in your lifetime. Someone decides they selfishly want something or to get ahead in life in some capacity, and they have no problem going after it at the expense of other people. Obviously, what took place in this story was not just at the expense of the head coach. Players, coaches, and parents were used as pawns to achieve this unethical man's desires. And running ill-conceived plays to bring about negative consequences demonstrated he had no regard for the success of the team or its budding athletes. God's Word is not devoid of such characters, so let's investigate one such individual to uncover some valuable insights.

On the Run

In 1 Samuel 20, we learn that Jonathan struggled to believe that his father, King Saul, sought to take the life of his beloved companion and brother-in-law, David. However, it did not take long for Jonathan to undeniably learn of his father's death wish for David. During the second day of the new moon feast, Jonathan tried to verbally defend his distraught friend before his father, and the king erupted in violence and hurled a spear at his own son "to strike him down" (v. 33). So once Jonathan confirmed his father's murderous intentions toward David, the two tearfully parted ways. David had become an enemy of the state and fled for his life.

David desperately needed help, so he went to the sanctuary at Nob a couple of miles from Saul's capital city of Gibeah. David surely knew the goodness of the High Priest, Ahimelech, who oversaw the sanctuary, and felt confident he would receive some sort of aid. Paul, over a millennium later, commented that God's people should "engage in good deeds to meet pressing needs" (Titus 3:14). David was counting on that this holy man had fully embraced this principle. His needs were not only pressing, they involved his survival.

> Then David came to Nob to Ahimelech the priest; and Ahimelech came trembling to meet David and said to him, "Why are you alone and no one with you?" David said to Ahimelech the priest, "The king has commissioned me with a matter and has said to me, 'Let no one know anything about the matter on which I am sending you and with which I have commissioned you; and I have directed the young men to a certain place.' Now therefore, what do you have on hand? Give me five loaves of bread, or whatever can be found." The priest answered David and said, "There is no ordinary bread on hand, but there is consecrated bread; if only the young men have kept themselves from women." David answered the priest and said to him, "Surely women have been kept from us as previously when I set out and the vessels of the young men were holy, though it was an ordinary journey; how much more then today will their vessels *be holy*?" So the priest gave him consecrated *bread*; for there was no bread there but the

bread of the Presence which was removed from before the Lord, in order to put hot bread *in its place* when it was taken away. Now one of the servants of Saul was there that day, detained before the Lord; and his name was Doeg the Edomite, the chief of Saul's shepherds. David said to Ahimelech, "Now is there not a spear or a sword on hand? For I brought neither my sword nor my weapons with me, because the king's matter was urgent." Then the priest said, "The sword of Goliath the Philistine, whom you killed in the valley of Elah, behold, it is wrapped in a cloth behind the ephod; if you would take it for yourself, take *it*. For there is no other except it here." And David said, "There is none like it; give it to me" (1 Samuel 21:1-9).

The author artfully infused several tension-builders in this scene, as he set the stage for the continuation of this story in the next chapter, where he brings to light Saul's irrational and dark thought world. As David approached Ahimelech, the priest's imagination must have been running wild. "Why is David here and alone?" "Where are his servants, his soldiers?" "Is it true what others have reported about Saul pursuing David to Naioth in Ramah?" "Surely not, he is the king's loyal son-in-law and commander of his guard!" "But why is he by himself?" "He looks tired and bewildered." "Surely something is amiss." "Might Saul follow him here?" "This cannot be good...not good at all." The priest's insecurities caused him to start physically trembling as he walked up to the Goliath-killer, and as we will see in 1 Samuel 22, his trembling was most certainly warranted.

Desperate for food and needing to calm down the anxious priest, David concocted a story that he was on a secret mission for the king. David's deceit accomplished its purpose, but unknowingly, plowed some dangerous ground for Ahimelech. Some scholars believe David was not lying if "the king" in his account was God.[25] However, this still was deceit. Ahimelech would not have interpreted David's tale in such a way. As we shall see, by not telling the truth to the unsuspecting priest, he placed Ahimelech in a precarious position with Saul.

David continued his web of deceit and convinced Ahimelech to give him the week old "bread of the Presence" that had been replaced with hot bread on the Sabbath. This bread was normally reserved for the priests (Leviticus 24:5-9), but Ahimelech felt that he was keeping with the spirit of the Law by compassionately providing the consecrated bread to the needy David. Jesus implicitly applauded Ahimelech's benevolent approach to this circumstance before a group of Pharisees over a thousand years later (Matthew 12:1-7).

You've met this character. Whether on a movie or TV screen, in a book, or even in real life, you "know" this devious type. Skulking in the background, around corners, outside windows, and in adjacent rooms, such people maliciously eavesdrop and observe people of interest. With their newfound knowledge, these miscreants sell out their victims. They are opportunists, willing to provide their information—distorted or straight—to others for acceptance, rewards, promotions, money, good standing, and the like. As we shall see, such was Doeg.

To the Hebrew reader, the aside that introduced Doeg would have set off a screeching alarm in their heads. "Uh-oh, something is awry. What is this no-good 'Edomite' doing at the Sanctuary... watch out David!" Edom was a longstanding enemy of Israel. They would not let the Israelites pass through their land during Israel's wilderness wanderings (Numbers 20:14-21). Saul even led his nation into battle against Edom (1 Samuel 14:47). Perhaps Doeg was captured during one of their skirmishes, and after discovering his usefulness, Saul may have found the Edomite quite valuable and enlisted his services.[26] Introducing Doeg as "the Edomite" suggested a sinister presence was at work in Nob. Doeg was "Saul's" servant and was surely ready to report to the king anything associated with David and his whereabouts.

Presenting Doeg as "the chief of Saul's shepherds" may help

us understand why he was "detained before the Lord" at Nob (v. 7). As Saul's head herdsman, Doeg may have brought a delivery of lambs to the priests for future offerings.[27] Unfortunately for the Edomite, he may have arrived after the Sabbath was underway as suggested by the availability of the consecrated bread, which was replaced by "hot bread" on this sacred day. The priests may have refused to inspect the sheep until the Sabbath was over thus detaining Doeg.

Interestingly, right after Doeg's introduction, David sought a weapon from the priest. We learn later from 2 Samuel 22:22 that David must have seen the Edomite lurking in the background. Perhaps David thought he might need a sword or spear to fight his way out of Nob. In Psalms 52, David referred to Doeg as a "mighty man"…an *evil* mighty man." Doeg, like David, was an accomplished warrior as well as a shepherd. As part of Saul's court, the "fugitive" David knew Doeg well, and he was keenly aware that he was in the company of a shrewd and formidable opponent. David evidently felt his life was in peril because of Doeg, as he immediately "fled that day from Saul" (v. 10). But the young David now had a prized battlefield trophy hanging at his side: the sword of Goliath.

Despicable King, Despicable Follower

In the next scene, the whole story will turn on Saul's madness. He no longer can properly discern right from wrong. His reasoning is unsound. His judgment has become fatally flawed. Irrational conspiracies are now this self-centered king's norm for making sense of the world. Any desire he once had to seek and accomplish God's will has left him. His hatred for David has consumed and twisted the inner depths of his soul. Once a proud king, Saul has turned into a broken-down figure with an attitude of "woe is me" burdening his heart.

Then Saul heard that David and the men who were with him had been discovered. Now Saul was sitting in Gibeah, under the tamarisk tree on the height with his spear in his hand, and all his servants were standing around him. Saul said to his servants who stood around him, "Hear now, O Benjamites! Will the son of Jesse also give to all of you fields and vineyards? Will he make you all commanders of thousands and commanders of hundreds? For all of you have conspired against me so that there is no one who discloses to me when my son makes *a covenant* with the son of Jesse, and there is none of you who is sorry for me or discloses to me that my son has stirred up my servant against me to lie in ambush, as *it is* this day." Then Doeg the Edomite, who was standing by the servants of Saul, said, "I saw the son of Jesse coming to Nob, to Ahimelech the son of Ahitub. He inquired of the Lord for him, gave him provisions, and gave him the sword of Goliath the Philistine" (1 Samuel 22:6-10).

Picture the scene, David and his men were spotted, so Saul called together his close advisors to discuss the matter. Imagine that you were one of those Benjamite confidants of Saul. After Saul queries as to whether you believe that the Judean David would bless you like he had done, he then questions your loyalty, believing that you have conspired against him. You are ready to defend yourself, when you notice the spear in Saul's hand. The spear with which the crazed king tried to "pin David to the wall" on more than one occasion (1 Samuel 18:11; 19:10). The spear that he hurled at Jonathan so that he could "strike him down" (1 Samuel 20:33). The spear that may come your way if you say the wrong thing. Since the king has turned into an irrational, depressed, conspiracy theorist, perhaps silence is your ally. So you zip your lips and let the lunatic rave.

A non-Benjamite loomed in the background amongst Saul's confidants that day. He heard Saul espouse the gifts of "fields and vineyards" and positions of authority he gave to his loyal Benjamite brethren. As an Edomite, Saul's accusations were not aimed at him. His opportunity to ingratiate himself with the king was at hand, so he stepped forward, and not only told what he knew of the "son of Jesse" (derogatory way to refer to David), but indicted Ahimelech in the matter, as well. To help us make sense of a key part of Doeg's allegation, let's look at the rest of the passage.

> Then the king sent someone to summon Ahimelech the priest, the son of Ahitub, and all his father's household, the priests who were in Nob; and all of them came to the king. Saul said, "Listen now, son of Ahitub." And he answered, "Here I am, my lord." Saul then said to him, "Why have you and the son of Jesse conspired against me, in that you have given him bread and a sword and have inquired of God for him, so that he would rise up against me by lying in ambush as *it is* this day?" Then Ahimelech answered the king and said, "And who among all your servants is as faithful as David, even the king's son-in-law, who is captain over your guard, and is honored in your house? Did I *just* begin to inquire of God for him today? Far be it from me! Do not let the king impute anything to his servant *or* to any of the household of my father, for your servant knows nothing at all of this whole affair." But the king said, "You shall surely die, Ahimelech, you and all your father's household!" And the king said to the guards who were attending him, "Turn around and put the priests of the Lord to death, because their hand also is with David and because they knew that he was fleeing and did not reveal it to me." But the servants of the king were not willing to put forth their hands to attack the priests of the Lord. Then the king said to Doeg, "You turn around and attack the priests." And Doeg the Edomite turned around and attacked the priests, and he killed that day eighty-five men who wore the linen ephod. And he struck Nob the city of the priests with the edge of the sword, both men and women, children and infants; also oxen, donkeys, and sheep *he struck* with the edge of the sword (1 Samuel 22:11-19).

After Saul summoned Ahimelech and all the priests at Nob, Saul again went down a path of unreasonableness. In Saul's earlier tirade, "all" of Saul's advisors had "conspired" against him (v. 8), now Ahimelech joined the party and was accused of conspiracy as well. But Ahimelech's supposed collusion occurred directly with the hated "son of Jesse," which did not bode well for the high priest. Saul accused Ahimelech of aiding an enemy of the state by providing him provisions, a weapon, and even inquiring of the Lord for the "outlaw."

Ahimelech's defense was short and to the point. He stated to Saul that David was known for his loyalty, as well as being "your son-in-law," "captain over your guard," and an honorable member of your household—all perfectly valid points unless your king has turned into a raving lunatic who vehemently hated David. And, of course, such niceties concerning David would have just added fuel to Saul's burning rage.

In verse 15, the high priest claimed absolute innocence in the whole affair and declared he knew nothing of David's alleged crimes. Ahimelech commented directly on the accusation that he consulted God for David in the first part of this verse: "Did I *just* begin to inquire of God for him today? Far be it from me!" (v.15). Some scholars interpret this as a declaration rather than a question, which would imply that Ahimelech admitted to consulting God for David. However, from the context and allowing Psalm 52 to shed some light on this verse, one could deduce that Ahimelech was asking a question to aid his argument as to his claim of innocence. Robert Alter astutely proposes that Ahimelech was conveying the following: "I never previously consulted the oracle for David, and why on earth would I do it now?"[28]

We cannot fully know what Doeg actually saw and heard at Nob, but I believe we can make some strong conclusions concerning this matter. First, the narrator totally left out any mention of Ahimelech's consulting God for David. If it was an oversight, it would be a major one. I believe he left it out because it did not happen, and it adds to the despicable nature of Doeg in the story that the author was trying to convey. Second, if David did ask Ahimelech to seek advice for him from God, what would he ask him? David had fabricated a ruse to get rations and a sword from Ahimelech, thus any question would need to go along with the deception and would have been pointless.[29] In fact, even under his duress, it's hard to fathom that David would have God consulted with a fictitious question. Third, by Ahimelech declaring his innocence in regard to querying God for David, this would correspond well with his following statement of blamelessness. Fourth, Psalm 52 is attributed to David and speaks to his thoughts concerning Doeg, which were quite angry thoughts, indeed.

> Why do you boast in evil, O mighty man?
> The lovingkindness of God *endures* all day long.
> Your tongue devises destruction,
> Like a sharp razor, O worker of deceit.
> You love evil more than good,
> Falsehood more than speaking what is right.
> You love all words that devour,
> O deceitful tongue (Psalms 52:1-4).

David thoroughly and artistically called Doeg a liar. Doeg's deceptive words resulted in destruction and devoured human life. To David, Doeg was evil to the core.

Doeg, through his opportunistic lies, hurled Saul into a rage. Doeg knew it would. The sacrilegious Edomite had no problem in achieving some of his personal goals at the expense of others. This opportunist's lies resulted in the death of all the priests, their families, and their animals, except Ahimelech's son, Abiathar, who escaped to David. When Saul's own guard refused to kill the "priests of the Lord" at his command, "the Edomite," and assuredly his own band of warriors, struck down the priests and then their city. Doeg revered neither the Lord nor His priests, so

Saul took advantage of his evil nature. Yes, Doeg was sinister—lethally sinister.

When Abiathar fled to David's camp, Israel's future king took responsibility for the massacre of Ahimelech's household. David knew that Doeg would run to Saul and reveal what he had seen. But surely David was surprised at Saul's reaction. To kill God's priests was an affront to God and utterly evil, even if it had been incited by a lie. No, David was responsible for lying; Saul and Doeg were responsible for murder. Perhaps David learned a valuable life lesson from this incident, as we see in his earnest words in the following psalm.

> Set a guard, O Lord, over my mouth;
> Keep watch over the door of my lips
> (Psalms 141:3).

I think you would agree with me that all of us need to seek God in this regard on occasion, as situations arise where we may be tempted to spin a little deceit.

As with David's ruse, lying often brings about unexpected consequences and can take unpleasant turns for all involved. My family owns a couple of timeshare weeks and frequently make trades to go to somewhere in the Blue Ridge mountains. On one occasion, after arriving at one of our favorite resorts in the high country of North Carolina, the sales staff started badgering us to attend a presentation about this location and some of their other resorts around the country. We resisted the temptation of the free gift card on the first two inquiries, but after the third call, I had a weak moment and agreed. They assured me that it would only take 30 minutes, and I even double-checked on the time commitment. Their talk was scheduled on the fourth day of our stay, and up to that point, rain had plagued our plans throughout our vacation. As we walked into the presentation room, I started to regret my decision, because the sun started to peek out from behind the clouds. The speaker's enthusiasm and the content of the presentation kept me engaged, but when the 30-minute mark hit, my eyes started to repeatedly stray to the beauty of our surroundings through the windows. After 45 minutes, the salesman switched tactics and started to denigrate another timeshare company of which many of us were members. I wasn't there to hear him belittle someone else's program but to hear about the quality of theirs. As the clock ticked onward, an uneasy tension started to take hold of me. A lie about the length of the presentation lured us away from our vacation time, and I felt they were taking advantage of our good will. The minute hand struck the hour mark, and the speaker continued to drone on with no end in sight. I momentarily lost it and stood up amid the audience and bellowed out, "You all lied to us! You said this would only take 30 minutes!" Needless to say, "startled" only began to describe this poor salesman's reaction.

Their lie incited me. No one likes being taken advantage of through deceit. It is quite upsetting. Their lie led to their salesman's pitch falling apart. They, in turn, had no sales that day. To his chagrin, no one had made the salesman aware of the 30-minute promise. I became a hero to the other attendees that day. I received accolades from them through the rest of the week, because they felt taken advantage of as well. Nevertheless, my momentary outburst raised my stress level for the remainder of the day. A lie directly contributed to my demeanor taking an ugly turn, and I regretted that it had occurred. No, I was not a hero; I was just an upset victim of a liar who sadly allowed a deceptive sales practice to change my mood. Deception by a member of the sales staff to boost attendance produced a number of unexpected outcomes—and none of them were good.

In hindsight, David surely wished he had asked God how he should have handled the situation he faced with Ahimelech. David's lie contributed to a horrific outcome. With such a heavy burden hanging over him, we can understand his appeal to God to "set a guard" over his mouth. Let's develop hearts with a good Christian ethic and seek God whenever possible to help us develop the appropriate words of truth to achieve our aims. After all, we are people of truth.

Parting Thoughts

Most likely, we all have witnessed the negative impact of an opportunist. You may know of an individual who took advantage of the right circumstances to achieve his or her thoughtless goals. Nothing much matters to them when the right opportunity presents itself. The destructive wake they generate devours whoever or whatever lies in its path. At the expense of people, the environment, relationships, and other things, they uncaringly press forward to satisfy their selfish desires. Hopefully, you have never encountered anyone as sinister as a Doeg who exhibited such ruthless behavior. Nevertheless, this attitude to a lesser extent can develop in our hearts and definitely goes against the caring ways God desires for us to possess. Let's look at a few examples to better understand how this attitude may be affecting each of us.

When I was in various positions of leadership at NASA, one of my responsibilities included evaluating candidates for promotions and selecting the most qualified. Those candidates were keenly aware when such opportunities were approaching, so some of them started behaving in ways to assure their accomplishments were noticed. They understood these promotions were competitive and wanted to make sure management knew of their desirable attributes, capabilities, and achievements. A lot of this occurred in constructive ways, such as through conversations, notes, logbook entries, and often just through paying attention to the normal course of business. Regrettably, not all of their tactics were above board. Some of these hopeful contenders decided to try to gain an advantage at the expense of their competition. When the opportunity arose, they privately made sure that I was aware of one of their competitor's shortcomings. This was usually done in a subtle manner, though not always. So rather than standing on the quality of their own merits and qualifications, they chose to try to bring another employee down a notch or two in my eyes. Thankfully, I tended to see through such antics and recognized it as a character flaw on their part. I must admit though that some people are quite artful at this method of self-promotion.

When my son graduated from college and started his first job, I gave him some advice that relates to the above. I told him to create *value* in himself in his company's eyes. To do this I recommended the following strategy. He needed to thoroughly understand exactly what his company expected of him and then perform at a high level in that regard. As it came to the skills needed to do his job, he should hone those capabilities through added training and self-study to excel in these areas. He needed to make his company profitable through his wise and efficient use of his time and their money (or a customer's money). When problems arise, he was obligated to make sure they were solved in a timely manner, so deadlines could be met. And he needed to have the foresight to predict where his company was headed, so he could develop the future skills that would be required of him. I ended by saying, "If layoffs ever come, make it an extremely hard decision for them to let you go because of your value to the company."

We need to all develop the type of character that allows our qualifications to stand on their own when it comes to potential promotions. Demeaning others in a subtle or blatant way to gain an upper hand in this process is un-Christian. And when it comes to the shortcomings of others at work, management will typically discover those over time. We do not need to point them out. We need to excel at what we do and care about our co-workers while letting Christ be seen through our actions.

Another character flaw in this vein involves making fun of

others or putting them down in an effort to endear ourselves to our friends and colleagues. Acceptance becomes a paramount concern for some of us, and we sometimes slip into poor behaviors in an effort to achieve it. A little light banter with one another is often an amenable part of a relationship, but at times, things can go too far and get out of hand. To show how funny or clever we are, our joking can turn hurtful. We may want to impress others, but such conduct actually shows our cruelty. Generally speaking, we need to use language that builds others up, not tears others down. Take note of the positive aspects of our friends and their achievements, and when the time is right, compliment them on those things that are praiseworthy. Always be genuine, and your comments should be well-received.

I had a friend who really struggled with complimenting other people. If he were present at a gathering of my friends, he started fidgeting when we praised another's accomplishment. He almost always interrupted the praise to tell of some remarkable achievement of his own. He wanted our approval, so he tried to displace someone else's positive attention by seeking his own. Compliments should easily roll off our lips Paul told the Corinthian church that when *"one* member is honored, all the members rejoice with it" (1 Corinthians 12:26). Not only is this a good principle to follow in our churches, but it is worthy to follow throughout all aspects of life. Learn to be happy for the achievements of others if it is truly praiseworthy, and let those compliments flow.

Jesus shared the parable of "The Pharisee and the Publican" to distinguish two different ways one might approach God in prayer. The Pharisee's was unacceptable, while the tax-gatherer's was acceptable.

And He also told this parable to some people who trusted in themselves that they were righteous, and viewed others with contempt: "Two men went up into the temple to pray, one a

Pharisee and the other a tax collector. The Pharisee stood and was praying this to himself: 'God, I thank You that I am not like other people: swindlers, unjust, adulterers, or even like this tax collector. I fast twice a week; I pay tithes of all that I get.' But the tax collector, standing some distance away, was even unwilling to lift up his eyes to heaven, but was beating his breast, saying, 'God, be merciful to me, the sinner!' I tell you, this man went to his house justified rather than the other; for everyone who exalts himself will be humbled, but he who humbles himself will be exalted" (Luke 18:9-14).

The Pharisee's prayer was at the expense of the tax-gatherer before God, at least in his own view. In the Pharisee's mind, the tax-collector's occupation made him contemptible, and when compared to him, God was lucky to have a righteous person like himself as one of His own. Perhaps we should more accurately say, "self-righteous." His self-proclaimed "righteousness" came from comparing his ways against others' shortcomings. Therefore, he recognized no sinful ways or attitudes in his own life. In reality, he needed just that for which the tax-gatherer cried out humbly: mercy. A truly righteous Pharisee would have also asked for God to help the tax-collector overcome the temptations he faced within his occupation and allow him to be a healing influence in the tax-collector's life.

Lastly, consider a character flaw that typically exhibits itself in the trivial things of life, but by constantly giving in to its ignoble tendencies, it may show up in weightier matters, as well. Most exercise facilities ask their customers to not "hog" one of the exercise machines. Maybe not in those words, but it is typically posted as one of their rules of etiquette. Some people though have no consideration for others. So at the expense of not letting other people complete their workouts in an expeditious manner, they sit on a machine between repetitions or leave their towel on the machine as if to say, "Reserved. Stay off." Perhaps these folks never learned to share their toys as a child and have continued this practice in their adult years. If someone needs to use a machine for a moment, and you have to reconfigure the machine to satisfy your needs, so what! Take turns! Life kind of works that way at times. Such inconsiderate attitudes also come to the forefront on our highways, in parking lots, and in the grocery stores. You've seen such behavior. We need to think about how our actions may affect others. And when it may be detrimental to their interests, consider behaving differently and in a caring manner. Such is the lot for those who are to "love your neighbor as yourself" (Matthew 22:39).

Questions

1. Why did David lie to Ahimelech? How did it create a dilemma for Ahimelech? How might David have approached the situation with Ahimelech differently?

2. How does the author shape our view of Doeg throughout the scenes we investigated? Do you believe Doeg was an opportunist? If so, how did he go about it?

3. How do you view Saul's character in the passages discussed? How did he view David?

4. Do you think Doeg took advantage of Saul? If so, how?

5. Have you ever been taken advantage of by an opportunist? In what ways? How did that make you feel?

6. Perhaps not as sinister of Doeg, but do you have any attitudes within you that cause you to try to achieve your desires (whether great or small) at the expense of others? How should you deal with such a character issue? How might you approach achieving your desires differently?

7. Discuss some lesser venues where you see others going after their desires at the expense of others? How do you view such activities? Do you believe they can escalate into something more serious down the road?

CHAPTER 6

Herod Antipas

People-Pleasing
and Preposterous Promises

**How can you believe, when you receive glory from one another
and you do not seek the glory that is from the one and only God?**

(John 5:44)

One of my favorite TV shows is *American Pickers*. I really enjoy watching Mike and Frank go across the United States in their van looking for "rusty gold," as they like to call it. Their searches take them from dilapidated barns to well-organized buildings that house somebody's lifelong collection. For those two treasure hunters, they prefer rummaging through old stockpiles of dusty and dirty stuff, because they know that no one has gone through them for a long time. They uncover some remarkable antiques and relics from the past; some in good shape, some not so good. To the untrained eye, many of their rediscovered finds are in horrible shape and appear to be worthless, but they understand the value that may still exist to different types of collectors and those who are skilled at restoration.

Mike and Frank are depicted as two fun-loving characters who appear to enjoy each other's company. A lot of friendly banter constantly goes on between the two. In one episode, Mike was bragging about all the raw oysters he could eat at one sitting. Frank had finally heard enough and challenged his oyster-loving buddy to live up to his outlandish claims. Mike affectionately referred to Frank as the "bearded-charmer," so Frank promised to shave off his cherished beard if his partner could eat six dozen raw oysters at one meal. Servers delivered tray after tray of oysters-on-the-half-shell to Mike. He started to slow down a little but kept putting them away. While the restaurant's staff and many customers gathered around him and cheered him on, the engorged picker swallowed his 72nd oyster. As the place went wild and Mike cherished his gluttonous feat, Frank sat there dejected and in disbelief, knowing the unpleasant obligation he must honor.

The scene switched to the next morning, and a disheartened Frank sadly prepared to shave off his beloved beard. When his razor started down his face, a tear also rolled down his cheek. Perhaps dramatized or staged, this story illustrates what can happen when we make rash and ill-conceived promises to others.

By not thinking through the details and the potential outcomes of a promise, an unexpected result may place a burden on our shoulders that we did not see coming. Such were the consequences of some preposterous promises (or oaths) that we see in God's Word. Let's take a close look at one incident that clearly exhibits this principle.

Herod the Not-So-Great

During the time of John the Baptist's and Jesus' ministries, Herod Antipas served as the tetrarch (regional ruler) of Galilee and Perea for the Roman Empire. His father, Herod the Great, King of Judea, bequeathed this responsibility to him, and he carried out this role from 4 BC to AD 39. Antipas had apparently married King Aretas's daughter to create good will with his Nabatean neighbors on Perea's southern border. It was a calculated move that later backfired. During a trip to Rome, Antipas fell in love with his half-brother Philip's wife, Herodias. Desiring to marry her, Antipas honored Herodias's request to divorce the Nabatean princess before she would consent to the marriage, and this "not-so-great" move set off an unexpected consequence. Once Aretas's daughter made her way back to her father, this aggravated an already tenuous relationship between the two territories and contributed to a border war that resulted in the destruction of Antipas's army. Rome had to intervene to suppress the Nabatean threat.[30]

Coinciding with the divorce, the actual decision to marry Herodias was "not-so-great" either. Whether Antipas realized it or not, he had chosen to marry a headstrong and evil woman comparable to Jezebel. This marriage kicked off a series of events that created a lot of problems for the weak, cruel, and morally corrupt Antipas. Since Mark provided the more detailed account of John the Baptist's unfortunate demise, let's utilize his Gospel for our study and fill in a few blanks with Matthew's version.

> For Herod himself had sent and had John arrested and bound in prison on account of Herodias, the wife of his brother Philip, because he had married her. For John had been saying to Herod, "It is not lawful for you to have your brother's wife." Herodias had a grudge against him and wanted to put him to death and could not *do so*; for Herod was afraid of John, knowing that he was a righteous and holy man, and he kept him safe. And when he heard him, he was very perplexed; but he used to enjoy listening to him (Mark 6:17-20; see also Matthew 14:1-12).

The bold John the Baptist made sure that the Jewish Antipas knew that he stood in violation of God's law by marrying his sister-in-law (Leviticus 18:16; 20:21). With his half-brother still alive, such a marriage would be considered adulterous and scandalous to his Jewish subjects. In fact, since John's rebuke was repetitive (note in v. 18, "been *saying*"), it pointed to the abhorrent nature of this wayward leader's offense. Herodias had heard enough, and she wanted John put to death for his insolence. According to Matthew's account, Antipas "wanted to put him to death," as well (Matthew 14:5). However, even though Antipas probably did not enjoy listening to John's accusations, he had more significant worries. Josephus recorded that Antipas's concern was not one of religious morality, but rather political survival. He wanted John executed because he feared his accusations could precipitate a rebellion.[31] Through John's prophetic preaching that the coming of the Messiah's kingdom was at hand, some of the Jewish populace might have been stirred to a feverish pitch.[32] And with John's accusing their supposed "Jewish" leader to be an unrepentant lawbreaker, Antipas realized that he had a politically dangerous situation on his hands. He knew quite well that such a repeated accusation could be interpreted as a call to overthrow him.[33] Nevertheless, his initial "not-so-great" solution to put John to death might have triggered what he desperately was trying to avoid in the first place (Matthew 14:5). The attraction of the Jewish people to the wilderness prophet created a fear in Antipas that an uprising might occur if he chose to execute him. Antipas was also afraid of John himself, not because he was prone to violence or sedition, but he knew that John was a righteous and holy man of God (v. 20). So he took a less fearful route and threw God's prophet in prison at Macherus to repress his accusations and keep him safe from the clutches of vengeful Herodias.

Have you ever come across a speaker who had the ability to draw you into his message, keeping you riveted to every word of his presentation or message? John the Baptist appeared to have had such an effect on Antipas. He not only enjoyed listening to him, but the prophet's words left him "perplexed." John's prophecies and ethics left the curious leader in a quandary. His faith (or lack of) was challenged. A conflict arose in his reasoning. He questioned whether he should pursue God's way or his own self-serving, shameful lifestyle? Such dilemmas can be spiritually healthy, as we evaluate who we are, where we are heading, and what God desires for us. Unfortunately, John's message just left this conflicted leader "perplexed"—in a state of "I don't know what to do." What a miserable place to live!

The Outrageous Oath

As we peer into the details of John the Baptist's execution, the reality comes with a chilling force. Extravagance, corruption, and ineptitude rule the day in this segment of Antipas's life. Set up as a dupe, Herod "the not-so-great's" warped inner character came to the forefront and cost an innocent man his life.

> A strategic day came when Herod on his birthday gave a banquet for his lords and military commanders and the leading men of Galilee; and when the daughter of Herodias herself came in and danced, she pleased Herod and his dinner guests; and the king said to the girl, "Ask me for whatever you want and I will give it to you." And he swore to her, "Whatever you ask of me, I will give it to you; up to half of my kingdom." And she went out and said to her mother, "What shall I ask for?" And she said, "The head of John the Baptist." Immediately she came in a hurry to the king and asked, saying, "I want you to give me at once the head of John the Baptist on a platter." And although the king was very sorry, *yet* because of his oaths and because of his dinner guests, he was unwilling to refuse her. Immediately the king sent an executioner and commanded *him* to bring *back* his head. And he went and had him beheaded in the prison, and brought his head on a platter, and gave it to the girl; and the girl gave it to her mother. When his disciples heard *about this*, they came and took away his body and laid it in a tomb (Mark 6:21-29).

You may ask, "Why classify Antipas as a dupe?" Because Mark appears to imply that Herodias shrewdly deceived him to achieve her wicked goal of bringing about the death of John the Baptist. To her, Antipas's predictability made him an easy target for her to ensnare. So what actually happened that would lead us to conclude that the beguiled tetrarch was duped? Other explanations are possible, but several elements of the story suggest that hate-filled Herodias subversively had planned John's murder. Mark recorded that Herodias not only carried a "grudge" against the law-quoting prophet, but she deeply loathed him to the degree that she wanted him killed (v. 19).

A grudge is not a passing disgruntled notion. Its evil talons penetrate our wounds and leave a gaping hole that does not heal. Vengeance festers and waits for an opportune moment to strike and "get even." So when Mark reported that "a strategic day came" (v. 21), the events to follow were not happenstance, but the tactics of a grudge-driven woman intent on fulfilling her murderous ambition.

Some scholars believe that Herodias would never have sent her teenage daughter before a bunch of partying men to perform a dance. However, when you consider the moral depravity of Herodias and Antipas, along with her desperate and unrelenting hatred of John, such a move by Herodias would not be out of the question. And knowing her husband, she knew that a seductive dance by Salome (Herodias's daughter through Philip)[34] would be the crucial feature of her scheme to entrap her depraved husband.[35] The text does not specifically state that Salome's dance was sensuous, but again, the raucous activities that accompanied parties of this sort, and the boisterous oath of Antipas could certainly lead one to such a conclusion.[36] Here are a few typical comments from some acclaimed scholars concerning the nature of Salome's dance: "The undoubted implication of the text is that the dancing was sensual,"[37] "The dance was unquestionably lascivious,"[38] "...captivates him with her presumably erotic dancing,"[39] and "A dance such as referred to here at a banquet of drunken men would have been a suggestive and sensual event."[40] Actually, birthday parties were considered pagan celebrations by the Jews, and such a dance by Salome would not be out of place at such an event.[41] Whatever the case, we can unequivocally say that the dance extremely captivated Antipas and his fellow revelers.

Another aspect of the story that suggests that Herodias staged the whole affair was the immediacy of what followed Antipas's extravagant and "not-so-great" oath. For instance, Salome left the banquet hall at once to go talk to her mother. No discussion transpired with her mother about the possibilities of her request. In fact, she came back "immediately" and "in a hurry" to make her mother's request of John's head. Salome offered no repugnance regarding her mother's grizzly proposal. Actually, the fulfillment of the oath had nothing to do with what Salome wanted, but was solely to bring about her wicked mother's desire. Herodias made sure that Antipas did not attempt to weasel out of the murder of John by asking that his head be brought to her on a platter, so she could verify that her husband followed through with the request. She insisted that this happen "at once" (v. 25); rather than at a later time. What a way to end a party.

Whether Herodias planned the whole ordeal or not, Antipas placed himself in a precarious position by making such an outrageous oath. Perhaps with his judgment affected by alcohol and a seductive dance, the tetrarch's impaired state contributed to such a preposterous promise: "Whatever you ask of me, I will give it to you; up to half of my kingdom." This proverbial expression of extreme generosity indicated that he would go to great lengths to honor her request.[42] Obviously, such a rash and grand gesture would leave anyone open to problems if it were followed by a truly grandiose request. Christians are people of truth, and our words are, in essence, promises (Matthew 6:33-37). Therefore, we must thoroughly think through any offers we make to others, such as partnering with them on a business venture, loaning them large amounts of money, committing an excessive amount of our time to some project, or even making obligations within our families that we may not be able to fulfill. We cannot control the future. Such commitments can destroy relationships, throw us into financial ruin, and potentially entice us to cross ethical and moral lines. So before making a "preposterous promise," talk it over with loved ones and trusted knowledgeable confidants. Let time be an ally as you wisely anticipate the consequences of such a commitment, and whatever you do, keep control of your faculties while making such decisions.

People-Pleasing

One of the saddest aspects of this story involved Antipas's response to Salome's gruesome request. Yes, he was "very sorry" (v. 26). And yes, "he was grieved" (Matthew 14:9). But do not feel sorry for this self-serving, weak-kneed ruler because he was led astray by a scheming wicked woman. He had within his power to refuse to put John to death in spite of the oath. Yet, to pacify or impress a bunch of drunken revelers, Antipas murdered an innocent man; "…because of his oaths and because of his dinner guests, he was unwilling to refuse her" (v. 26). Another "not-so-great" decision. Rather than continue down a path of evil, Jewish rabbis had developed ways to release the Jewish people from ill-conceived oaths.[43] Sparing the life of a guiltless man would have surely fallen within the spirit of those exceptions. Not that this "supposed" Jew paid any attention to their laws, but executions without a trial and beheadings were against it.[44] It's a sad day when one ignores his religious training and chooses to commit atrocities for the sake of others.[45] Antipas may have been sorry about making the oath, but he wasn't sorry enough.

We have probably all made rash judgments about a personally disturbing situation and boldly claimed that we would deal with it in some aggressive fashion. As we started down our war path, additional information came to light that should have caused us to change our original course of action. In order to maintain our supposed "honor" in the eyes of others, we proceeded anyway to use our misguided tactics and inappropriately handle the situation because of our foolish bravado. That's a "false sense of honor."[46] It's actually dishonorable. Attempting to escape ridicule we do the ridiculous. Sometimes we just need to eat a little bit of crow. Let's profess that we rushed to or had a lapse of judgment and apologize if necessary, then change our strategy and deal with the circumstance in a godly way.

Many of us have said, "I don't care what others think," but

typically, we do. Who wants others to think ill of us or be openly ridiculed? To avoid this, we may behave in ways to seek the approval of our friends, relatives, and colleagues. Trying to please others for the sake of acceptance can lead us into making foolish decisions and acting in non-Christian ways. For example, you desire to grow closer to a particular friend, and to achieve this, you agree to participate in an ethically questionable activity. Or, you want to be accepted by a group of colleagues, so you enter into a conversation knowing that it contains immoral undercurrents and actually offends your conscience. And on another occasion, you just remain silent to give others the impression that you agree with them on some morally shady position. Why do we want to grow close to others who cannot accept us for who we are and what we believe? We should not live our lives as a masquerade. If we must practice questionable behaviors for others to accept us, we need to question our motivations and what truly is important to us.

Perhaps the attitude of one of our astronauts can help us a little with our thinking here. Music holds a special place in the heart of astronaut Carl Walz. He has participated in his church's music ministry since he was 17. At the time of his Expedition 4 mission to the International Space Station (ISS), he performed as the lead singer for the astronaut rock band Max-Q (Max-Q is the point where maximum dynamic pressure is encountered on a vehicle during atmospheric flight). So there was no way that Carl could leave planet Earth without addressing such a love. Consequently, he kitted a piano keyboard and some sheet music with his personal belongings.

Carl's Sunday routine typically included singing hymns and other Christian music. The lyrics to many of these songs hold deep-meaning and life-shaping power for him. One of the hymns he enjoyed singing during his ISS stay was "Be Thou My Vision" and stated the following on how this song touches him.

...especially the lines, 'Riches I need not, nor man's empty praise, Thou mine inheritance, now and always.' That always runs through my mind...and whenever I get discouraged I think of that, and it's like, well, who cares what people think? It's what God thinks that's important.[47]

Carl truly got it right! Let's learn to seek what's important to God, and let that help shape our attitudes and reveal any misguided motivations that may produce poor behaviors. Acceptance by God always trumps acceptance by others.

A Sad Commentary

Toward the end of Jesus' earthbound ministry, John provided a discouraging summary that not many people believed in Him, even though "He performed so many signs" (John 12:37). The beloved apostle then proceeded to give us what appeared to be good news at first, only to dash our spirits with a tragic commentary.

> Nevertheless many even of the rulers believed in Him, but because of the Pharisees they were not confessing *Him*, for fear that they would be put out of the synagogue; for they loved the approval of men rather than the approval of God (John 12:42-43).

Like Antipas, the desire for the "approval of men" again brought about a distressing outcome. Unlike Antipas, this group of people "believed" in Jesus. Or in other words, they had some sort of faith in Him, though shallow it may have been. Please understand, to "be put out of the synagogue" would be a tragic and scary consequence for a Jew. Along with being separated religiously, you would be ostracized socially. Financial devastation would also surely follow. Nicodemus thoroughly understood this, as he came to Jesus at night to avoid detection by wary onlookers (John 3:2). John identified Joseph of Arimathea as a "secret" disciple "for fear of the Jews," and this "prominent member of the Council"

(Mark 15:43) surely counted the costs before coming to Pilate to ask for Jesus' body in order to properly bury Him (John 19:38). Nicodemus joined Joseph in this bold endeavor.

What a sad state in which to find oneself; to actually believe in Jesus, only to refuse to "confess Him" because of the need for acceptance. The group of "believers" John mentioned "*loved* the approval of men" (my italics for emphasis) more than "the approval of God." I hope you noticed that they "loved" the approval. Their problem was not only grounded in fear but what they ultimately loved. Where the synagogue should have facilitated the development of a "love" for the "approval of God," it sadly created a "love" for the "approval of men." We face a similar dilemma. What do we love? Has our faith developed to the point where we would accept the rejection of some of our friends, colleagues, and relatives for the "approval of God?" We need to count the costs. Not all of those who are close to us will reject us, but we do run that risk. We must all understand how profound God's love is for each of us, so we, in turn, can also develop a deep love for Him.

> This is how God showed his love among us: He sent his one and only Son into the world that we might live through him. This is love: not that we loved God, but that he loved us and sent his Son as an atoning sacrifice for our sins (1 John 4:9-10, NIV).

"Church," please be inclusive and richly love on one another. Help develop the love of God in one another's hearts. Recognize that seeking the approval of those in the world may still powerfully influence many of our brothers and sisters. Let them see the love of God flow through us. Let them experience genuine Christianity. Hopefully, they still love their friends, but optimistically, the love for their approval will be displaced by the love of God's. Please do not be confused; it's not about them "seeking" our approval. God has already accepted them in His church, so they need our love and inclusion. Help them to understand that our acceptance of them is a natural outflow of the Christian walk, not something they need to seek. So let's graciously walk alongside one another and grow together in the love of God.

> Therefore, accept one another, just as Christ also accepted us to the glory of God (Romans 15:7).

Parting Thoughts

Let's go back and cover the verses that kicked off Mark's story of John the Baptist's execution so that we may glean a little more from Antipas. Before revealing the details of John's death, Mark exposes us to Antipas's agitated thinking, as he reflected on who this miracle-worker Jesus actually was.

> And King Herod heard *of it*, for His name had become well known; and *people* were saying, "John the Baptist has risen from the dead, and that is why these miraculous powers are at work in Him." But others were saying, "He is Elijah." And others were saying, "*He is* a prophet, like one of the prophets *of old*." But when Herod heard *of it*, he kept saying, "John, whom I beheaded, has risen" (Mark 6:14-16)!

Just a short aside, Mark's reference to Herod Antipas as "King" was probably a bit of irony. As mentioned previously, Antipas was a tetrarch—the regional ruler for the Roman Empire of the Perean and Galilean territories. Nevertheless, Herodias passionately desired the title of king for her husband, so she induced him to go to Rome and request it from Emperor Caius. While asking for the kingship, information was made available to Caius that Antipas had concealed a large armory, enough to outfit 70,000 soldiers. Concerned about a potential revolt, Caius removed the tetrarchy from Antipas and banished him and Herodias to Gaul.[48] By the time Mark wrote his Gospel, this would have already taken place. So ironically he used this title as perhaps a bit of sarcasm, as the "want-a-be" king discussed with others who the "King of kings" actually was.

In all likelihood, Antipas's religious beliefs were syncretistic, or in other words, his religious views were probably a hodgepodge of more than one set of beliefs. For example, he had Jewish instruction as a youth, he was educated in Rome, his first wife was Arabic, and as we discussed earlier, he liked to listen to John the Baptist. Also, the location he selected for his capital city and palace, Tiberias, was on the site of an ancient cemetery. It was an unlikely place for a practicing Jew to settle due to the unclean nature of the land.[49] Therefore, Tiberias's populace would have largely been composed of individuals with pagan beliefs. Antipas had some Jewish underpinnings, but he was likely influenced over the years by the various superstitious beliefs to which he had been exposed.

In Antipas's superstitious mind, the "miraculous powers" performed by Jesus required some sort of divine origin. He most likely believed that these powers were divinely given to Him by whatever god resurrected John in order to cause him trouble for unjustly executing the innocent prophet. Please note that Antipas was experiencing a guilty conscience. We can make this deduction because of his own declaration of guilt concerning John the Baptist: "whom I beheaded" (v. 16). Antipas murdered an innocent man against his better judgment. He executed a "righteous and holy man" (v. 20) as a result of an outlandish promise after being entertained. He had a blameless man beheaded, even though he could have recanted his oath but chose to look "honorable" before his guests. His conscience created the sorrow and grief that he experienced after Salome's request, but the weak-kneed king didn't heed it. To him, it seemed likely that John was back to haunt him in some form or fashion for his unjust deed.

The conscience is a remarkable tool that God has given humanity. We can train it for good purposes and allow it to have a righteous influence on our lives. Paul knew the criticality of a properly trained conscience for the Christian life, when he told Timothy, "But the goal of our instruction is love from a pure heart and a good conscience and a sincere faith" (1 Timothy 1:5). The conscience can be a beacon for godliness, but if not trained in righteousness, it can take us down sinful paths. Paul warned Titus of the dire results that come from a corrupted conscience.

> To the pure, all things are pure; but to those who are defiled and unbelieving, nothing is pure, but both their mind and their conscience are defiled (Titus 1:15).

Even if we train our consciences in godly ways that does not guarantee that we will follow them. As I am sure you have experienced, the lure of some temptations overwhelm the better judgment of our consciences, and we give in to some desire, only to regret it later.

For the remainder of this lesson, let's explore what happens when we go against our consciences. A lot of material is available to help us train our consciences, so let's spend a little time thinking about what happens when we choose a course of action that goes against a righteous conscience.

The most obvious result from not following our consciences is *guilt*. We often know the right course of action to take in a given set of circumstances, but choose not to follow it. I remember stealing a candy bar from a drug store when I was about 8. I ran outside with it and downed it so fast that I probably never tasted the delicious chocolate. Need I say, this went sorely against my conscience's leading. Even as an adult, this still haunted me. So a number of years back, I sent that drug store a letter of apology and $10 to cover the cost of the candy bar—plus inflation. My mind never let go of what had been so deeply ingrained into my conscience: Thou shall not steal. So I asked for forgiveness of God and those I offended and made things right the best way I knew how. I am so thankful for having a mother and father who instilled in me, when I was a child, the many godly ethics that to this day still reside deeply within my conscience.[50]

Guilt provides us with an important mechanism to let us know that we may need to make something right with someone, God, or both. Living in guilt can bring about shame and depression and cause us to not like ourselves much. God asks us to love others as ourselves, but that's hard to accomplish when we don't even love ourselves because of our past poor conduct. Let's ask for forgiveness from God, and others when appropriate, and then forgive ourselves. If possible, we need to make things right when we have wronged someone, but we then need to let things go, learn from our mistakes, and move on in life. If they do not want to forgive us, we cannot control them. What more can we do?

Going against our consciences awakens the ultimate thief and steals our peace. When we follow a righteous conscience, we can experience the peace that God intended for us. Walking blamelessly with our Lord is a wonderful existence. But when we go against a righteous conscience, guilt quickly erupts. This guilt can consume us. Jesus' blood allows us to be innocent in God's eyes and maintain a holy relationship with Him. In genuine repentance, turn to that blood and be forgiven. Stop carrying the guilt. God has forgiven you; forgive yourself.

Another consequence of going against a righteous conscience is *sorrow*. We have all probably experienced a situation in which our consciences set off an alarm within us to not choose a particular path. As clumsily as a bull in a china shop, however, we do or say something mean-spirited, leaving a hurtful mess in our wake. We may not have meant to hurt anyone, nevertheless, we momentarily lost control and our ill-conceived actions negatively affected them. We may also feel remorse before God for being involved in a sinful activity. Tearfully saying the words, "I'm sorry. I am so so sorry," is a heavy burden, but thank God for giving us a conscience that leads us to such a healing action.

Again, compromising our consciences gives rise to an exemplary joy-stealer. God wants us to experience joy in our Christian walk, but constantly violating our consciences is a sure fire way to lose it. Joy results when we lead a life of loving God and loving others. The Soggy Bottom Boys surely got it right in the lyrics to their famous song, "I Am a Man of Constant Sorrow." In one verse they express, "For six long years I've been in trouble, no pleasures here on earth I found." Joy will always flee from us if we choose to pursue the sinful things of life, and we'll head into a constant state of misery that sorrow and guilt bring.

One of my Christian friends struggled for many years with a self-indulgent lifestyle. Most people who were casually acquainted with him did not know that he constantly wrestled with this problem, but those who encountered him or tried to walk alongside him during his times of depravity often got hurt in some way. When he woke up from his sinful episodes and realized the pain he had caused others, a deep sorrow overwhelmed him as he recognized that these were the people who genuinely cared about him. He realized that he was driving away those who loved him, but his vile desire controlled him and placed him in a horrible cycle. When he finally got the help he needed and regained a healthy footing in life, one of the first things he did was seek out everyone he had hurt so that he could apologize. By doing so, he not only mended those relationships the best he could, but he healed himself from within. Joy re-entered his life and has remained.

Another friend of mine once told me that he believed that nothing was wrong with any particular behavior as long as it did not hurt anyone else. Obviously, there are some inherent issues with such a belief, but let's focus on one of them. Life has taught me that pretty much everything we do can affect others, even those things done in private. For instance, what we choose to get involved with will typically affect our moods and demeanor, which, in turn, will likely impact how we treat those around us. Our life experiences create biases, likes and dislikes, and will affect how we view others and behave toward them. Most certainly, those things that violate our consciences can throw us into guilt and despair and thus set our tone as to how we interact with our friends, relatives, and associates. Our quality of life and those around us will be impacted by many of our choices in life.

Lastly, let's consider fear as an aftereffect of violating a righteous conscience. Because of what we get caught up in, we may fear God. We may fear punishment. We may fear the authorities. We may fear how others will view us. We may fear how others will treat us. We may fear how life will change based on our poor choices. Fear. Fear overwhelms and consumes us. Again, our conscience remains a helper. Such fear reminds us to be accountable. The world may not need to know what we have done, but we need to be accountable to those we have wronged—whether God or man. God does not want us to live in fear. He wants us to live fearless in His love. You must understand that God loves us. He sent Jesus to redeem us, so we can have a relationship with Him. And as we walk in His loving light and ways, Jesus' blood is there to cleanse us of our sins (1 John 1:7). Such love produces love, and we want to constantly abide in that love. So stand accountable to God, and confess your sins to Him. As John said, "He is faithful and righteous to forgive us our sins and to cleanse us from unrighteousness" (1 John 1:9). Believe this, practice this, and don't live in fear but abide in His rich loving ways. Walk in His light my friends and a mutual love will develop between you and our amorous God. He already loves you. Yes, you!!!

> There is no fear in love; but perfect love casts out fear, because fear involves punishment, and the one who fears is not perfected in love (1 John 4:18).

Praise God for giving you such a marvelous tool and helper as your conscience. It may serve to flag you when you misstep, but try to keep it clear. Paul admonished his young apprentice, Timothy, to "fight the good fight, keeping the faith and a good conscience" (1 Timothy 1:19). God ultimately desires for us to keep it clear and in good shape. Train it righteously, and let it serve to reward you, not to punish you.

Questions

1. Why did Herodias and Herod Antipas want John the Baptist executed? Why did Antipas decide not to kill him? What did he wind up doing?

2. Leading up to Antipas's outrageous oath, do you think he was duped? How did this occur? What's your view of the overall situation?

3. Do you think it was "honorable" for Antipas to stick to his oath he made to Salome? How should he have handled this situation?

4. Have you ever made a preposterous promise?
What was the result?

5. What types of behaviors might we exhibit to gain the acceptance of those in the world? What can we do as the church and individual Christians to help fellow believers overcome the desire for the "approval of men?"

6. Have you ever violated your conscience? What occurred within you afterward? How does our conscience serve to help us after we violate it?

8. How should we deal with the guilt, sorrow, and fear that result from compromising our conscience?

CHAPTER 7

Demetrius

Inciting and Instilling

Love…does not act unbecomingly; it does not seek its own,
is not provoked, does not take into account a wrong suffered.

(1 Corinthians 13:5)

My father moved our family to Titusville, Florida, during the year that the National Aeronautics and Space Administration (NASA) was established. The space race was underway, and he wanted in on the excitement of helping our nation lead the world in utilizing and exploring space for peaceful purposes. Since I was only a year old at the time, I did not appreciate my father's zeal. He was a patriot through-and-through and proud to contribute his skill set to this noble endeavor. Being raised in Titusville came with a few perks, especially since the Kennedy Space Center and Cape Canaveral Air Force Station were just across the Indian River from our quaint little town. Even though I saw a lot of launches through the years, they never became commonplace. Watching those rockets soar through Florida's gorgeous blue skies was not only an exhilarating experience, but each of those technological achievements came with an inherent beauty. And the night launches…WOW! The plumes from those powerful rocket engines lit up the whole sky to our east; producing some exciting times for sure.

When I was a sophomore in high school, the program on which my dad had worked for a number of years was coming to an end. His company was willing to transfer him to another job in Denver, Colorado, but unfortunately, my mother had developed a crippling case of rheumatoid arthritis. On the advice of her doctor, they became extremely concerned about the cold climate of Denver and how it might aggravate this painful and debilitating disease. My dad decided to take a layoff and search for another job locally. Regrettably, he only had a two-year engineering degree, and all the companies at that time were only hiring engineers with four-year degrees. Even though my dad had the experience and knowledge that many of the companies desired, their hiring policies stood in the way of bringing on board a man to do a job that he had been successfully performing for years. This realization took a heavy toll on my father, and consequently, he became distant and worried.

Months passed, and my father still could not find a job that made him happy and satisfied. His unemployment started to have a direct impact on our family. My mother's arthritis kept her from seeking employment, but at 16, I knew what I needed to do. I had a friend who helped me get a part-time job at Sears, yet that came at a cost. For the first time since I had started playing baseball at age 8, I did not play. Other aspects of our family life also began to be impacted, such as the elimination of our yearly family vacation, going out to eat, buying certain types of food, and the like. Nevertheless, our love for one another ran deep, and if anything, this trial only served to deepen that loving bond.

My dad eventually found a meager job that he never really enjoyed, but an inner peace replaced the anguish he was experiencing because he desperately sought to provide for his family. We never had to suffer through the horrors that poverty brings on many in this world, but nonetheless, that was a stressful time, especially for my father. Strangely, sometimes even the good things in life can come with adverse effects. Such was the case as the fledgling church rapidly grew in the city of Ephesus during the first century.

The Good News and Its Impact in Ephesus

Power resides in the gospel message. Jesus' cross-work, along with God's accompanying resurrection activity, provides humanity with a true hope of an everlasting relationship with their loving God. Paul eloquently and succinctly made this statement concerning the gospel, "...it is the power of God for salvation to everyone who believes..." (Romans 1:16). Taken in its simplicity and purity, the gospel's message can radically impact our hearts. We need not impede its strength by burdening it with unnecessary traditions and church doctrines. Paul and his missionary partners experienced tremendous success in Asia Minor by converting many of the idol worshipers to Christ. In fact, the numerical response to the gospel message was so great that it even started to impact the livelihood of some of the trades. Let's look at what occurred in the proud city of Ephesus.

> About that time there occurred no small disturbance concerning the Way. For a man named Demetrius, a silversmith, who made silver shrines of Artemis, was bringing no little business to the craftsmen; these he gathered together with the workmen of similar *trades*, and said, "Men, you know that our prosperity depends upon this business. You see and hear that not only in Ephesus, but in almost all of Asia, this Paul has persuaded and turned away a considerable number of people, saying that gods made with hands are no gods *at all*. Not only is there danger that this trade of ours fall into disrepute, but also that the temple of the great goddess Artemis be regarded as worthless and that she whom all of Asia and the world worship will even be dethroned from her magnificence." When they heard *this* and were filled with rage, they *began* crying out, saying, "Great is Artemis of the Ephesians!" (Acts 19:23-28)

The massive and beautiful Temple of Artemis, one of the seven ancient wonders of the world, was in Ephesus. Erected on a platform of 240 x 420 feet, the temple spanned an area of 165 x 345 feet, which is approximately the size of a football field, including the end zones. Elaborately adorned, this colossal structure consisted of 127 marble columns extending to 60 feet high and carried the honor of being the largest building in the Grecian world.[51] Enshrined in the temple was an image of the goddess Artemis who was believed to have fallen from the sky and was possibly a meteorite (ref. v. 35). As such, the Ephesian worshipers of Artemis claimed that her image came directly from Zeus and was not fashioned by human hands. Containing such a revered sacred object, Ephesus held the title of "guardian" (also referred to as "temple keeper" or "temple warden") of Artemis's temple (see v. 35). Artemis of Ephesus was the mother goddess of fertility, and her image had some semblance of a multi-breasted female. Thousands of worshipers made pilgrimages to the temple each year to pay homage to Artemis, as well as to attend the weeklong festival devoted to her each spring. Believed to have the protection of Artemis, the temple also served as a bank for merchants, royalty, and even cities.[52] For many reasons, the Temple of Artemis became a major attraction for Ephesus and served as a boon to their economy. Obviously, their religion became intimately intertwined with their economy and culture.

Paul and his ministry team's success in bringing former idolaters to Christ had produced a spiritually healthy outcome. Their changed lives started to adversely impact Ephesus's economy. These new Christians were no longer purchasing small shrines and other goods associated with the idolatry trade. From Paul's teachings, they had learned the following about the nature of God and idols.

> Being then the children of God, we ought not to think that the Divine Nature is like gold or silver or stone, an image formed by the art and thought of man (Acts 17:29).

> Therefore concerning the eating of things sacrificed to idols, we know that there is no such thing as an idol in the world, and that there is no God but one (1 Corinthians 8:4).

Demetrius's silversmith business was off, and he understood why. The demand for his small silver shrines from tourists and worshipers declined due to the influence of Christianity. He wanted to "nip in the bud" the threat of this upstart religion on his livelihood.

At first glance, I felt a little empathy toward Demetrius and his tradesmen, because their ability to provide for their families was at risk. Yet, Demetrius's approach to addressing the problem was ruthless. In my life, the rapid advancement of technology has made many products obsolete. Eight-track tape players came and went in the blink of an eye. Rotary phones died out at the onset of the digital age. Except in professional baseball, wooden bats are a thing of the past. I see all these items nowadays in antique stores. We could go on and on with more diverse examples. Today's businesses need to try to forecast what is coming on the horizon and learn to adapt to remain viable. Nevertheless, flexibility was not in Demetrius's blood, and he had no intention of adapting to any changes. In some regards, the Temple of Artemis reminds me of Disney World and its impact on Florida's economy. If anything occurs that might adversely influence the tourist traffic associated with the Disney properties, all sorts of vendors, hotel chains, politicians, and developers start to flex their influential muscles to protect their financial interests. Perhaps many things have not changed much in the last couple of millennia.

Covert Inciting

Let's take a look at Demetrius's approach to solving the "Christian problem." His initial step was to gather his fellow craftsmen together to illicit support and a group response. First on the agenda, and of primary importance to Demetrius, was fear-mongering. Basically, his message emphasized that their prosperity depended on worshiper and tourist dollars associated with the Temple of Artemis, and if Paul kept teaching about this "Jesus," they could kiss their source of income goodbye. You can practically hear him saying, "And if they believe in this radical's teachings, why would anyone want to buy a shrine of a god who is actually not a god at all? Our trades will become obsolete!"

Demetrius then proceeded to the second part of his strategy. Since he had already imparted a fear for their future prosperity, it was time to turn that fear into rage, which would spur them into action. He accomplished this by revealing two additional potential impacts due to Paul's teachings that involved their religion. First, the beautiful and world renowned Temple of Artemis would be viewed as a worthless relic of a debunked religion. Second, the great Artemis herself would be dethroned and rendered as a non-existent deity. Pointing out a threat against their livelihood, along with an attack on their religion was a surefire way to stir up his comrades. Like a pack of rabid dogs, they furiously started chanting, "Great is Artemis of the Ephesians!"

Like Demetrius, some people are artists at stirring others into a frenzy. They know what makes us tick and rubs us the wrong way, as well as how to use this to incite us. Especially when they want us to do something, they bore right into those touchy areas. God's Word makes it quite clear that His people should not harbor anger and ill-will toward others (Matthew 5:21-24; Ephesians 4:26-27). As a corollary, a Christian should never intentionally provoke a brother or sister to be angry with others. Corruption resides in a heart that would desire to create in another person an attitude that is contrary to God's will.

A number of years ago, one of my friends dropped in on me unexpectedly. Something was troubling his heart, and he wanted my thoughts on the matter. For some time, he had wanted to use his skills to serve his church in a given capacity. Unfortunately, what he specifically wanted to do was against the wishes of one of the church's elders at the time. He then met up with a couple of other men who were perpetually unhappy with things at this church, and the conversation turned ugly. They vehemently thrashed out what was wrong with their church's leadership. He shared with me some of their concerns, and then proceeded to the core purpose of his visit. His question to me was short and *not* sweet: "Mike, I want to tear apart our eldership and start over. What do you think?" From past experiences, I knew the elders at his church, and my perception was that these were good and holy men, most certainly qualified to hold the office of an elder. I explained that to him and told him that he should repent of such an attitude and pursue more constructive approaches to address his concerns. I also told him to quit talking with those men who stirred him up since nothing good could come of such negative, bitter conversations. We discussed a few possible ways for him to approach his specific issue and prayed. As he left, his heart was in a much healthier place.

Demetrius's leadership qualities were quite lacking and even disturbing. He could have explored a number of other options before stirring up his colleagues. For one, he could have shared his concerns with the civil authorities and asked for their recommendations. With his fellow craftsmen, he may have explored other potential means to address their lack of sales, such as ways to better promote their merchandise or expansion into new products. Perhaps he should have looked into Paul's teachings to understand why so many people were converting to Christianity. Was it "the truth?" If so, should he continue to contribute to a false religion? Should he portray the situation in such a way that would deny the other craftsmen the opportunity to determine for themselves the validity of Christianity? Even a face-to-face talk with Paul might have helped him better understand what he was dealing with. Instead, Demetrius selfishly manipulated the craftsmen to head down a path that might lead to lawlessness and violence. Let's look at what happened next.

> The city was filled with the confusion, and they rushed with one accord into the theater, dragging along Gaius and Aristarchus, Paul's traveling companions from Macedonia. And when Paul wanted to go into the assembly, the disciples would not let him. Also some of the Asiarchs who were friends of his sent to him and repeatedly urged him not to venture into the theater. So then, some were shouting one thing and some another, for the assembly was in confusion and the majority did not know for what reason they had come together. Some of the crowd concluded *it was* Alexander, since the Jews had put him forward; and having motioned with his hand, Alexander was intending to make a defense to the assembly. But when they recognized that he was a Jew, a *single* outcry arose from them all as they shouted for about two hours, "Great is Artemis of the Ephesians" (Acts 19:29-34).

Demetrius had created the response he desired. Leaving the guild hall in a rage, the craftsmen spilled out onto the streets of Ephesus, inciting their fellow citizens to join them in their outrage. As a mob scene erupted, they feverishly desired to get their hands on Paul. Since he was nowhere to be found, they grabbed two of his missionary companions and drug them to an outdoor theater that held around 25,000 people. Typical of any unruly mob, tempers flare while chaos rules the day. Paul's companions faced a dangerous situation. Note how Luke emphasized the bedlam that prevailed: "The city was filled with the confusion," "some were shouting one thing and some another," "the assembly was in confusion," and "the majority did not know for what reason they had come together" (v. 29, 32).

Demetrius became silent. He could have quieted the crowd and brought some order to the riotous mob. Nevertheless, this dishonorable man's scheme had not come to fruition. He preferred the chaotic outcry to persist in hope of bringing out a city official. He wanted the city government's fingerprints on what happened next in their *ad hoc* assembly.

Concerned about being connected to the Christians, the Jews sent Alexander forward to convince the gathering that they were not associated with this "troublemaking" sect that followed Jesus. But as he tried to quiet the hostile crowd, they "recognized that he was a Jew" and proceeded to shout him down with an ongoing chorus of "Great is Artemis of the Ephesians!" To these followers of Artemis, the Jews were as bad as the Christians, because they did not recognize the deity of their goddess either.

Luke also accentuated how dangerous the circumstances had become. Paul wanted to go into the assembly to reason with the crowd and appeal to their good senses in an attempt to win the release of his companions. Perhaps as a Roman citizen, they would allow him to speak, and in Paul's mind, he might even use this as an opportunity to preach the gospel.[53] It wasn't that Paul didn't fear for his life, but he had the courage to place the situation in God's hands. Paul may have been referencing this event in his second letter to the Corinthians.

> For we do not want you to be unaware, brethren, of our affliction which came *to us* in Asia, that we were burdened excessively, beyond our strength, so that we despaired even of life; indeed, we had the sentence of death within ourselves so that we would not trust in ourselves, but in God who raises the dead; who delivered us from so great a *peril of* death, and will deliver *us*, He on whom we have set our hope… (2 Corinthians 1:8-10).

Some of Paul's converts recognized the desperate nature of this situation, and how things were deteriorating. They knew that some of the Ephesian populace might resort to violence under the circumstances. So as Paul sought to go into the furious fray of the theater, some of his converts prevented him from entering into this life-threatening setting. We need to appreciate this kind of concern for a brother or sister in Christ. When we recognize that they are about to step into a situation that may have dire consequences for them, let's allow our love to drive us into action and try to protect them from any undue harm.

Paul also received warnings from the Asiarchs to stay out of the theater. They also understood the serious nature of the whole affair and were concerned for the apostle's life. As a side note, an Asiarch was elected each year to a city where a temple resided in honor of the Roman emperor. The Asiarch official promoted loyalty to Rome and the worship of the Roman emperor.[54] As some of the Asiarchs were Paul's "friends," it speaks to the respectful way that Paul presented the gospel and treated others.

A Calming Influence

As the chant in honor of Artemis continued for two hours, someone with a little sense and a calm demeanor finally entered the riotous scene.

> After quieting the crowd, the town clerk said, "Men of Ephesus, what man is there after all who does not know that the city of the Ephesians is guardian of the temple of the great Artemis and of the *image* which fell down from heaven? So, since these are undeniable facts, you ought to keep calm and to do nothing rash. For you have brought these men *here* who are neither robbers of temples nor blasphemers of our goddess. So then, if Demetrius and the craftsmen who are with him have a complaint against any man, the courts are in session and proconsuls are *available*; let them bring charges against one another. But if you want anything beyond this, it shall be settled in the lawful assembly. For indeed we are in danger of being accused of a riot in connection with today's events, since there is no *real* cause *for it*, and in this connection we will be unable to account for this disorderly gathering." After saying this he dismissed the assembly (Acts 19:35-41).

Whereas Demetrius chose to incite others, the town clerk brought a calming influence to the gathering. Ephesus was a capital of a Roman province and considered a "free city." The town clerk served as the highest civic official in the city and was locally elected. He also functioned as a liaison to the Roman government.

As a local official, he was surely aware of the economic impact the growth of Christianity was having on his city, so his thoughts on their economic and religious concerns would go a long way among his constituents.[55]

Providing a legal perspective on the matter, the town clerk quickly brought some sanity to the ruckus that Demetrius and his malcontents had stirred up. He essentially said, "Think about it…these men have done nothing wrong, but you have! You know the Roman government does not allow us to have such 'disorderly gatherings,' and we could lose some of our 'free' status on account of such riotous activity." He also called out Demetrius by effectively saying (my words), "You know the legal means to address such issues, so use them, don't take matters into your own hands!" Though his faith was misguided, the clerk also appealed to the renowned and "undeniable facts" that Ephesus possessed the guardianship of the temple and the image sent from the gods that resided in it. He in essence communicated, "Your fears and worries are irrational, so 'you ought to keep calm and to do nothing rash'" (v. 36). After restoring order to the crowd, Demetrius's henchman released their grips on Gaius and Aristarchus. Viewed as innocent by the local government, these disciples freely left the theater unencumbered. Whereas Demetrius had a new worry, he could be held responsible by the Romans for instigating a riot. Such behavior could be viewed as seditious. His manipulative ways came back to haunt him.

Godly Instilling

Please note, Paul and his missionary team did not take on a campaign to remove Artemis worship from Ephesus; they sought to instill Christ Jesus in the hearts of individual Ephesians. Once these disciples started living transformed lives, they began to change some of their daily practices, which started to impact the culture and economy of their community. We need to believe that the gospel has this power—that God has this power. Perhaps at times, we need to attack head-on certain types of corruption in our communities. But most of the time, we just need to live transformed lives, teach the gospel to others, and by all means live it! Let's care about our friends, colleagues, neighbors, and relatives and perform good works in their lives that address real needs. Let them see Christ and the love of Christ in us. If we want to shut the doors to a strip club in our community, start winning to Christ the individuals who live there. Change in hearts will produce change in our communities. It worked in Ephesus. It can still work today.

Parting Thoughts

When I started down the road to conduct the ministry in which I am involved today, I struggled mightily trying to get established. I needed help from somebody who had faced similar startup difficulties in their ministries. A friend recommended to me a particular gentleman who definitely had the background to provide me with some relevant advice. I met with him, explained what I was doing, and in what capacity I needed his guidance. He said that he would offer me a little strategic direction, but it came with a condition. Elated that he was willing to provide me with some sage advice, I immediately tried to meet his stipulation. Unfortunately, what I tried to achieve for him ultimately failed (by no fault of my own), so he wound up not helping me. To be honest, it hurt. I wasn't hurt because he neglected to help me, but I realized that he manipulated me. I am not sure he even knew what he had done, but he had attempted to use me. He treated me like an object to attain something for himself with little regard to my feelings and needs.

At some point in life, most of us have probably tried to manipulate others or circumstances to get our way. Incidentally, some folks really excel at this. They are truly accomplished artists at the skill of manipulation. Many times, I've seen people succumb to their cunning tactics and happily choose a course of action that aligns with the manipulator's stealthy maneuvering. However, if they ever realize that they have been victimized by such clandestine tactics, a serious problem will follow. The hurt that I mentioned above typically turns into bitterness. I personally fought it for some time before I was able to let it go.

We should *care* about others as fellow human beings, especially our brothers and sisters in Christ. For us to covertly try to impose our will on others to achieve our goals is dehumanizing. We treat them as some "thing" that exists for the purpose of helping us attain our desires.[56] In doing this, we might sculpt our words like Demetrius to develop fear and incite passion. Manipulative language is often littered with half-truths, while strategically leaving out key facts, as the information is spun in such a way that does not allow the victims to make informed decisions and choices. Manipulation is definitely a self-serving way to deal with others.

Jesus asked us to "love one another" (John 13:34). Loving others involves providing them with the whole truth (except where confidentiality exists), at least as we understand it. Of course we will have our biases, but we should respect their need to make informed choices in life. Loving others never involves manipulating them. In fact, manipulation is directly opposed to how God wants us to treat them.

> Do nothing from selfishness or empty conceit, but with humility of mind regard one another as more important than yourselves; do not merely look out for your own personal interests, but also for the interests of others (Philippians 2:3-4).

Always remember how you felt when someone manipulated you in the past compared to when somebody took into account your best interests. God's ways will always leave us with superior results.

Paul intimately knew the importance of a peaceful existence to his evangelistic mission. With the lessons of the Ephesus riot in his past, Paul communicated to Timothy the following guidance, as his youthful missionary partner preached the gospel in Ephesus.

> First of all, then, I urge that entreaties *and* prayers, petitions *and* thanksgivings, be made on behalf of all men, for kings and all who are in authority, so that we may lead a tranquil and quiet life in all godliness and dignity (1 Timothy 2:1-2).

Paul was grateful. If not for the town clerk, all the mission work that they had accomplished in Ephesus could have been ruined. What had been a ripe mission field could have become an abandoned venture. He told the Roman Christians that a ruler serves as "a minister of God for you" (Romans 13:4). So he told Timothy to pray for those in authority that they might "lead a tranquil and quiet life" (v. 2). That's a prayer we should continue even today.

What result was Paul trying to achieve through this prayer? At first glance, we may think that he desired for Christians to live serenely and be at ease. Perhaps he hoped that would also be the case, but Paul's primary concern resided with the spread of the gospel. He revealed the rationale for this prayer in verse 4; for "all men to be saved and to come to the knowledge of the truth." Even in our own country, gunmen have entered church services and killed worshipers and seekers alike. And of course, this problem is magnified in many other countries around the globe. So yes, we need to pray this prayer today!

I think we all can relate to how turmoil within a church distracts its ministerial staff from spreading the good news. Unlike Ephesus, we usually do not rely on local authorities to step in because of external problems, especially since most of our issues occur internally. Divisive arguments concerning false teaching, church tradition, and even carpet color selection can all serve to sidetrack us from what is truly important. Nevertheless, atheists and other religions have become a formidable outside threat in recent years, as their aggressiveness to curtail the spread of Christianity in our society is at an all-time high. I recently saw an atheist wearing a shirt that said, "Let's take back Sundays!" Campaigns to remove public prayer, to remove references to the Christian faith in historic events, to remove Christian symbols from public places, to make our morals appear antiquated, and to legislate the taxation of churches are but a few of their devious activities. The misinterpretation by our courts of our right to the freedom of expression of religion has fueled their initiatives. Who knows what the future may hold as they continue their onslaught? Pray that our authorities will facilitate the spreading of God's truth, not impede it.

I was preaching part-time at a church plant several years ago. We started to outgrow the homes in which we were meeting, so we began to investigate alternative facilities that we could afford. One of our members came across a man who rented space in a commercial building, where he ran a restaurant for the people who worked there. Since he was not open during the hours we held classes and services, he asked us if we would be interested in subleasing his space during those times. He let us hold one of our services there on a trial basis to see if the environment would suit our needs. Besides moving a few things around before and after we met, the facility held great promise for us, so we excitedly pursued the possibility of subleasing the space from him. Regrettably, he got back with us in a couple days and told us that the owner of the building was a Muslim and would not consider allowing a Christian group to use it. Wow! We'd been shot down by religious discrimination. It was truly unexpected and disheartening! We momentarily discussed pursuing a lawsuit. We felt some law might protect our right to rent the space there. But at the same time, we did not want to waste the money or time fighting it, knowing it would distract us from our core reason for wanting to be there. We also felt that such a lawsuit might communicate a negative message to the community we desired to serve. So we quickly let go of the possibility of taking legal action. Our country has changed in some ways that make our mission quite challenging at times.

Please also note, that while leading our hoped for "tranquil and quiet" lives, others can observe how we go about this "in all godliness and dignity" (v. 2). Our behaviors should attract them to the gospel, not repel them. Let the appeal of our love, integrity, and general care for others shine brightly and draw others to the gospel message. Let's not only spread the gospel; let's live the gospel. Let's be the gospel.

Questions

1. What is meant by "there is power in the gospel?" How does this power manifest itself? Can we impede this power? Explain.

2. What was Demetrius's concern with Paul's teaching? What was his strategy to deal with it? How might Demetrius have approached the problem more constructively?

3. Has anyone ever tried to bring about fear or anger within you? If so, how did they go about it? How did you respond?

4. How did the town clerk go about calming the riotous crowd? What were his arguments? With what new worry did Demetrius have to be concerned?

5. Paul did not lead a campaign to remove Artemis worship in Ephesus, so what was his primary mission? What were the results?

6. Have you ever been manipulated by someone? If so, how did it make you feel? How does someone actually manipulate another person? What can we infer from God's Word concerning manipulation?

7. Why is it important for us to lead "tranquil and quiet lives in all godliness and dignity?" Should we pray this prayer today, why or why not?

CHAPTER 8

The Ten Spies
Faith of the Faithless

For we walk by faith, not by sight.

(2 Corinthians 5:7)

Several people have sought me out over the last several years to understand what led to my decision to take an early retirement from NASA and go into ministry. Believe me, such a decision came with a lot of careful forethought, contemplative prayer, relentless anguish, and some serious soul-searching. God thoroughly blessed me by allowing me to work for NASA. I often tell people that I did things in my career that some people would pay to do. My career involved many exciting opportunities, such as working on the Space Shuttle, the International Space Station, and planning for eventual human missions to Mars. Nothing was more exhilarating and rewarding though, than when we launched a Space Shuttle. When "the man" starts counting down from 10, a little adrenaline just naturally starts to flow. Yet on the other end of the spectrum, nothing was so heart-rending as the Challenger accident. Only a few things in my life had such a lasting effect on me as that horrible tragedy. Nevertheless, we persevered and restored the Shuttle fleet to flight status at the launching of the Discovery, and an overwhelming tearful joy flooded my heart on that marvelous achievement.

So why would I leave such an awesome job? One of my colleagues asked me this same question. He knew that I started to put a plan in place to leave NASA, and he wanted to know what in the world was I thinking. He asked, "Mike, you have so many wonderful job opportunities available to you at NASA, why would you ever leave? What's wrong?" Actually, something was right...very right. I told him, "God had put a new passion in my heart, and no matter what I took on at NASA, it was just not fulfilling." For me, not following God's purpose for my life brought on a sense of dissatisfaction. The only way for me to experience contentment was to pursue my newly found passion.

God reinforced this passion through three different facets of my life. First, several people shared some specific words of encouragement with me that started to grab my attention. At the conclusion of a Sunday morning Bible class I was teaching, one devoted member pulled me aside and said, "I want you to know that I've thoroughly enjoyed your class, and it is my all-time favorite." After preaching a sermon at my church, two separate individuals remarked, "Mike, you need to be doing this full-time." Following a major workshop, a kind woman mentioned to me, "Your sessions were the best ones at the entire workshop." Please understand that I share these comments not for my ego's sake, but I needed to process what these folks had collectively communicated to me. This encouragement came from a diverse mix of people in various settings. As I mulled over their combined remarks, I specifically remember the following thought that kept surfacing in my mind: *Perhaps it was time to start giving my God-given gifts, talents, and skills fully to God rather than NASA.*

The second facet involved the doors that God kept opening for me. For instance, NASA offered me the opportunity to look into how the Agency might provide spiritual support for astronauts on long-duration missions. Wow, what a remarkable assignment! As you might imagine, not only was this task extraordinarily unique, but such an assignment for a government worker bordered on the bizarre. I was totally dumbfounded when the subject was first broached. In fact, I looked at the senior manager who mentioned this possible area of research and said, "You've got to be kidding me!" I planted no hopeful ideas or in any way hinted at such an assignment, as this opportunity was the invention of an innovative NASA executive, and it was definitely a jawdropper. The project lasted two-years, and I learned about many astonishing stories concerning the faith of some of our astronauts.

Another door opened up for me through another job opportunity that fell my way. What the job entailed wasn't altogether noteworthy, but the hours required to perform it allowed me to undertake an important new pursuit. Not many of the jobs in my career could be accomplished in 40 hours a week like this one, since it had a lot of built-in flexibility. This allowed me to attend the Harding School of Theology and start working on a Master of Arts in Christian Ministry. Remarkably, the year I completed this degree program aligned with my daughter's graduation from college, our home being paid off, and NASA's offering early retirements with a small buyout that would leave us debt-free. We had some financial concerns because my pension would be reduced significantly with my leaving NASA early, and we were still paying quite a bit of money for my son's college expenses. Nevertheless, my wife and I felt we could fiscally handle the circumstances that faced us.

Lastly, I felt a strong sense of leading from God and His involvement in various aspects of my life. When you diligently pray over such new directions as I was entertaining, you should expect God's involvement and leading. I felt His guiding hand in a number of areas, such as what classes to take, areas of research to emphasize, books to read, people I should get to know, and activities in which to become involved. Perhaps the most amazing facet of God's involvement in my life came through honing my writing skills. When God wants you to do something for Him, He will prepare you as you pursue it. God introduced me to gifts that I didn't even know I had. He transformed some of my attitudes along the way as well. Today, I can truly say that I love libraries, and librarians…well, they are some of my favorite people. What a transformation!

As we considered all these many aspects as a whole, we could not deny God's involvement. He left His fingerprints everywhere. My wife and I felt all the aforementioned circumstances built a pretty sound case for taking an early retirement, but one more item kind of sealed the deal—21st Century Christian offered to publish my first book, *An Angel's View: Encountering God Through the Stories of the Heavenly Hosts*. To be honest, even with all that had occurred, we still had to step out on faith. My job at NASA provided us with a lot of security, and leaving the space program to which I had patriotically devoted many years of my life was scary on several fronts. Life would be forever different. We faced several unknowns. A dependency on God would become crucial for my success. So I faithfully followed the words that one of our astronauts expressed as he readied himself for liftoff: "I placed my fate in God's hands, put my fears away, and focused on the job ahead. The Creator had brought me here; now it was my turn to show that God's faith in me was well placed."[57] Now launched on a new trajectory, I pressed forward with no regrets and no looking back.

Stepping out in faith involves a great deal of trust in God. God's Word provides us with many stories of some phenomenal, faith-filled people who diligently followed God's desire for them. However, now and then, some of God's people stumbled in the face of what appeared to be insurmountable obstacles. Fear displaced their faith, and human reasoning removed God from the picture. Let's take a look at one such case that resulted in a bit of wandering.

Reminiscing About the Promise

Moses stood with his fellow Israelites on the brink of entering into the "Promised Land." God had brought them out of Egypt through an arduous wilderness to the southern border of the land of Canaan, and its conquest was next on the agenda. Perhaps during this momentous occasion, Moses took a few moments to muse over the history of God's promise to give to Israel a land "flowing with milk and honey." So join with me in a possible re-creation of this lauded leader's reminiscing. As Moses started to think about the land promise, he marveled over how long ago the promise had initially been made. God first made this promise to Abraham, when He told this man of great faith that the land of Canaan was to be given "to your descendants" (Genesis 12:5-7). Abraham later learned that this promise would not come to pass until his descendants suffered through a period of oppressive slavery that would last for 400 years in a foreign land (Genesis 15:13). God reaffirmed the land covenant with Abraham's son, Isaac (Genesis 26:3), and again with Isaac's son, Jacob (Genesis 28:13). Moses remembered how Jacob sought to escape the horrors brought on by a severe famine, so he moved his household to Egypt, where they could be provided for by his son, Joseph, who was a ruler in this nearby affluent land. Joseph, on his deathbed, assured his brothers that God would take care of them and return them "to the land which He promised on oath to Abraham, to Isaac and to Jacob" (Genesis 50:24).

Moses thought how the good fortune of God's people suddenly changed for the worse in the land of his birth. As the Israelites rapidly multiplied in Egypt, a king arose to power who had no ties to Joseph. He had assigned taskmasters over the Israelites and enslaved them. Their labor became increasingly harsh as the Egyptians "made their lives bitter with hard labor..." (Exodus 1:14). Moses's heart went out to them as he remembered how they cried out to God because of the severe nature of their bondage.

With his mouth slightly agape, he recalled the ominous encounter he had with God at the burning bush; "God had heard the prayers of His people and chose to powerfully act, and he made to me the following declaration."

> …I have surely seen the affliction of My people who are in Egypt, and have given heed to their cry because of their taskmasters, for I am aware of their sufferings. So I have come down to deliver them from the power of the Egyptians, and to bring them up from that land to a good and spacious land, to a land flowing with milk and honey, to the place of the Canaanite and the Hittite and the Amorite and the Perizzite and the Hivite and the Jebusite. Now, behold, the cry of the sons of Israel has come to Me; furthermore, I have seen the oppression with which the Egyptians are oppressing them (Exodus 3:7-9).

Moses never thought in his *wildest* dreams that he would become God's chosen leader to win the release of His oppressed people and lead them to the Promised Land. He paused in utter amazement, as he mused over how the Creator of all things worked with him and through him to perform so many extraordinary signs and miracles along the way. What a mighty God he served!

With the exodus from Egypt underway, Moses recalled that he specifically reminded the Israelites that the Lord would fulfill his promise to their forefathers and bring them into "a land flowing with milk and honey" (Exodus 13:5). To ensure their success, Moses recalled that on two separate occasions that God had told him that He would protect them along the way and give them victory when they reached the land by sending an angel to accompany them. Unfortunately, the second occasion came with a sorrowful stipulation, as God was upset with His people over making and worshiping a golden calf.

> Then the Lord spoke to Moses, "Depart, go up from here, you and the people whom you have brought up from the land of Egypt, to the land of which I swore to Abraham, Isaac, and Jacob,

saying, 'To your descendants I will give it.' I will send an angel before you and I will drive out the Canaanite, the Amorite, the Hittite, the Perizzite, the Hivite and the Jebusite. *Go up* to a land flowing with milk and honey; for I will not go up in your midst, because you are an obstinate people, and I might destroy you on the way" (Exodus 33:1-3; also see Exodus 23:20-23).

Moses considered his sojourning with these people and thought, *God's right! These people are horribly obstinate, but I have a divinely given job to perform. And even though they complain and grumble at times, I deeply care for them.*

With the "great and terrible wilderness" (Deuteronomy 1:19) behind them and the Promised Land before them, Moses put his memories aside and mentally tried to start preparing God's people for the conquest of the land by reminding them of what the Lord had done.

'See, the Lord your God has placed the land before you; go up, take possession, as the Lord, the God of your fathers, has spoken to you. Do not fear or be dismayed' (Deuteronomy 1:21).

God promised them the land. God did many remarkable things to bring them to it. Moses remembered, but would the people? In Moses's preparatory statement, did he foreshadow something about which he was deeply concerned with his people? We might ask, "Why bring up fear, Moses?"

Scouting Out the Land

Sometimes in life we need to understand what we are up against. A trusted friend who may be familiar with a particular situation may tell us to go ahead and do "such and such." They'll say, "Everything will be all right. Trust me." And we do trust them, but we want to check things out for ourselves. When undertaking difficult tasks, we might want to exercise a little due diligence. Prior to going in to conquer the land of Canaan, God's people approached Moses and asked if they could perform some reconnaissance of the territory before commencing with the conquest. Moses agreed that such maneuvers made sense (Deuteronomy 1:22-23). He must have then presented this plan to God and gained His approval, because in this account in Numbers, the Lord commanded Moses to "spy out the land of Canaan," by using a leader from each of the tribes (Numbers 13:1-2).[58] As a way of reminder, God again reassured Moses that "I am going to give to the sons of Israel" this land (v. 2). *Give* was the word they needed to embrace fully.

Before starting any military operations, Moses wanted to know what the landscape looked like, whether the people living there were formidable opponents, and if they would encounter fortifications. From the perspective of a full-scale occupation, he was also interested in the quality of the land for supporting them agriculturally, as well as the availability of trees. For 40 days, the 12 men performed their covert mission and thoroughly assessed the land and its occupants. When the spies returned to the Israelite encampment, some of the people's eyes probably gleamed with excitement, as they saw them carrying a huge single cluster of grapes. To keep from damaging the grapes, "they carried it on a pole between two men, with some of the pomegranates and the figs" (Numbers 13:23). Encouraging indeed!

When they delivered their report to Moses and Aaron, as well as to the entire congregation, they showed them the fruit and unanimously agreed that the land "certainly does flow with milk and honey" (Numbers 13:27). God told them this many times, now they validated it. Then the spies proceeded with their assessment of the people and the cities. No longer unanimous, the report turned gloomy.

> "Nevertheless, the people who live in the land are strong, and the cities are fortified *and* very large; and moreover, we saw the descendants of Anak there. Amalek is living in the land of the Negev and the Hittites and the Jebusites and the Amorites are living in the hill country, and the Canaanites are living by the sea

and by the side of the Jordan." Then Caleb quieted the people before Moses and said, "We should by all means go up and take possession of it, for we will surely overcome it." But the men who had gone up with him said, "We are not able to go up against the people, for they are too strong for us." So they gave out to the sons of Israel a bad report of the land which they had spied out, saying, "The land through which we have gone, in spying it out, is a land that devours its inhabitants; and all the people whom we saw in it are men of *great* size. There also we saw the Nephilim (the sons of Anak are part of the Nephilim); and we became like grasshoppers in our own sight, and so we were in their sight" (Numbers 13:28-33).

At first, the evaluation started out quite unsettling, though the people voiced no pessimism going forward with the conquest. Nevertheless, they clearly communicated that military maneuvers against large fortified cites, and the people of great stature who occupied them, would be quite challenging. Caleb understood their negative tone and nature of their words, so before they did any further damage, he decided to try to counteract their pessimism. With God's promise obviously in view, Caleb attempted to encourage those listening that they could "overcome" these hurdles (v. 30). In other words, God said He would "give" them the land, so why would they start disbelieving in Him at that point? He delivered them there like He said. The land flowed with milk and honey like He said. Come on folks; have a little faith!"

Unfortunately, the report then takes an extremely negative turn. Fear rooted out whatever faith in God the 10 spies had once possessed. Viewed from a human perspective, they respond with "we are not able..." (v.31). Perhaps we have uttered these exact words when facing tough situations. Please note, these difficulties were real. Caleb's faith came not through some form of blind optimism. Caleb saw these impediments, but his faith was derived through God's perspective, not through human frailty.[59]

The references to the sons of Anak, the Nephilim, and that the "land devours its inhabitants" communicated one key message; "These are violent and warlike people of great stature, and we stand no chance in taking over this land by combat." So they gave a "bad report" to Moses and the rest of the Israelites. Of course some of the inhabitants were large, but to say that "all" the people they saw were of "great size," and to describe themselves as grasshoppers was fear-filled exaggeration to discourage the listeners. Perhaps, they should have concerned themselves more with how God would view them rather than how the inhabitants would. Always remember, God can perform remarkable things through grasshopper-sized folk who have faith.

Grumbling and Blaming

If the faithless spies were trying to stir up the people to join them in their pessimism, they succeeded royally. Confronted with such a dreadful assessment, the Israelites immediately became panic-stricken and fearful. In their minds, an insurmountable obstacle stood between them and the Promised Land, so they started grumbling and lashing out at Moses and Aaron. Moses had a full-fledged mutiny on his hands.

> Then all the congregation lifted up their voices and cried, and the people wept that night. All the sons of Israel grumbled against Moses and Aaron; and the whole congregation said to them, "Would that we had died in the land of Egypt! Or would that we had died in this wilderness! Why is the Lord bringing us into this land, to fall by the sword? Our wives and our little ones will become plunder; would it not be better for us to return to Egypt?" So they said to one another, "Let us appoint a leader and return to Egypt" (Numbers 14:1-4).

Grumblers often fantasize the worst. Basically, that's the Israelites' ear-piercing message to Moses: "We're going to die!" Grumblers often become irrational. Hysteria had gripped the exodus sojourners, thus a return to slavery and to live under their old oppressive taskmasters became a viable solution in their minds. Grumblers, by nature, are spiritually immature or corrupted. Totally disregarding God's promise, these ancient murmurers blamed Him for their current predicament. You would think they would at least consider the following: "Is not the One who collapsed a wall of water on the Egyptian army capable of handling these pagans in the land of Canaan?" Over and over again, God told them He would give them the land, and He would destroy its inhabitants. Fear had replaced any semblance of faith, so they vehemently grumbled and pointedly blamed the Lord.

One of the church's persistent problems throughout the centuries is grumbling. When it gets going, it often spreads like a gasoline-fueled fire. Nothing good ever comes from grumbling. You can probably think back through the years and recall a few regrettable incidents that initially started out with some incessant grumbling. The following are a few generalities and some typical outcomes that can come from this despicable behavior. Grumbling by its nature will make us aggravated inside, and it typically inflames the attitudes of others as well. Thus, a chronic complainer leads a stress-filled life. Grumblers ignore the good in any circumstance that contains some feature that they dislike. Grumblers are blamers. They ignore the overall context of a particular incident to assign blame to somebody other than themselves. They never share in the blame, because they are good (or right) and others are bad (or wrong). Church leaders resign because of complainers. Ministers can be let go because of a group of grumblers' persistent complaints. Congregations become divided because of murmuring. Good Christians are hurt by a grumbler's vicious accusations. Where grumblers run rampant, membership dwindles because many Christians do not want to be a part of such a destructive environment. Grumbling is absolutely un-Christian.

Church leadership must put a quick stop to grumbling. Leaders need to set the tone of a congregation's environment to promote its spiritual well-being, and grumbling will always be a detriment to this. Leadership should avoid giving a grumbler a platform to speak publicly. They can give them an ear, but leadership must shift the tone of the grumbler's language to something more constructive, whenever possible. Too often, grumblers bully leaders into adopting their view on a particular issue. That isn't leading. Leaders, please help create a culture of loving speech in our congregations.

Paul asked the Christians in Philippi to do the following:

> Do all things without grumbling or disputing; so that you will prove yourselves to be blameless and innocent, children of God above reproach in the midst of a crooked and perverse generation, among whom you appear as lights in the world... (Philippians 2:14-15).

In other words, a surefire way to be blameworthy and guilty is to grumble and dispute things. Of course, we will disagree with one another over a number of things, and there will be incidents where a specific person may be at fault. But Paul does not want us to use inflammatory speech to address these type of situations. Even in difficult circumstances, we can use language that is respectful, loving, and constructive to address the issues at hand. Jesus did not say, "Blessed are the grumblers!" Grumblers promote dissension; peacemakers promote peace. Peacemakers are the "sons of God" (Matthew 5:9). And as Paul so aptly pointed out, it is these "children of God" that serve as "lights to the world." Please, be those lights!

Let's get back to Moses and his nation of grumblers. Rather than grumbling, one might have expected the Israelites to anxiously ask Moses to speak to God on the matter, since they had firsthand knowledge of the Lord's power to deliver them. Moses, as well, surely wanted to know what the Lord's approach would be for defeating these menacing adversaries, so seeking Him out on such a complication should have been just a natural turn of events. Regrettably, their grumbling contained three features that related to God: (1) They disregarded God's plan by wanting to go back to Egypt; (2) they desired to replace God's appointed leader to take them there; and (3) they blamed the Lord for taking them out of Egypt in the first place. I once heard someone say, "God could take the Israelites out of Egypt, but He could not get Egypt out of the Israelites."

Moses and Aaron "fell on their faces" after the people's brazen outburst against the Lord. Gordon Wenham astutely points out, "To fall on one's face is the Old Testament's ultimate mark of religious worship and awe, but in Numbers, it usually anticipates some great act of judgment."[60] Caleb and Joshua tried to reason with this unreasonable horde by reminding them of the Lord's promise and ability to deliver the land to them.

> ..." The land which we passed through to spy out is an exceedingly good land. If the Lord is pleased with us, then He will bring us into this land and give it to us—a land which flows with milk and honey. Only do not rebel against the Lord; and do not fear the people of the land, for they will be our prey. Their protection has been removed from them, and the Lord is with us; do not fear them" (Numbers 14:7-9).

Even the most rational, calm and eloquent speech by two godly men could not curtail their mutinous intent. Their fear and panic had already led to irrational reasoning, and now these unrestrained traits produced hostility against their faith-filled comrades. An already agitated gathering turned into a mob scene after these two righteous men spoke, as the rebels believed the views of these two optimistic spies would get them killed. So they stood ready to stone Joshua and Caleb. In a glorious and terrifying fashion, the Lord suddenly appeared in His fiery cloud above the tent of meeting to put a stop to their evil intentions (v. 10). Then, they truly had something to fear.

God was thoroughly disgusted with the Israelites. It's rather revealing to look at God's assessment of the Israelites over the entirety of His conversation with Moses and to take note of all the many negative comments He made about them: (1) they've spurned Him (v. 11, 23), (2) they do not believe in Him in spite of all the signs they've seen Him perform (v. 11), (3) they've put Him to the test (v. 22), (4) they've not listened to His voice (v. 22), (5) they're evil (v. 27, 35), (6) they grumbled against Him (v. 27, 29), (7) they've rejected the land (v. 31), (8) they were unfaithful (v. 33), and (9) they've made complaints against Him (v. 27). Ouch! What a disturbing list for the Almighty to rattle off against this wayward group. It's important to understand God's view of this rebellious nation, as He metered out a severe judgment. God had endured enough, and if not for Moses's intervention, God would have destroyed them (v. 12). Moses appealed to God's nature by prompting Him to let the surrounding nations see His great power to deliver on His promises, as well as to demonstrate His lovingkindness and mercy by forgiving the people (v. 13-19).

God relented and agreed to pardon them, but He would still hold them accountable for their actions. This rebellious lot would not be the foretold descendants to inherit the land; it would be their children. Thankfully forgiven, these grumblers would wander in the wilderness for the next 40 years, and ironically, would ultimately receive their grumbling plea to die "in this wilderness" (v. 2). Only two adults would enter the Promised Land, God's faithful spies, Caleb and Joshua, and these righteous leaders would be instrumental in its conquest. Over the next 40 years, the Lord had a little heart-work to perform to facilitate the development of a spirit similar to Caleb's in the hearts of those who chose to faithfully follow God. God's judgment against the 10 faithless spies was harsh. Their "bad report" directly attributed to the grumbling that rapidly spread across the entire Israelite congregation. Regrettably for the disbelieving 10, they all "died by a plague before the Lord" (v. 37). Such a dreadful conclusion should make us take special care never to start our fellow Christians down a path of grumbling.

God told Moses they were to return to the wilderness "by the way of the Red Sea" (v. 25). Hardheadedness typically accompanies hardheartedness, so of course, some of the Israelites decided they would go up and take the land, even though God had told them to do otherwise. Moses gave them an extremely stern warning to not proceed with such folly.

> But Moses said, "Why then are you transgressing the commandment of the Lord, when it will not succeed? Do not go up, or you will be struck down before your enemies, for the Lord is not among you. For the Amalekites and the Canaanites will be there in front of you, and you will fall by the sword, inasmuch as you have turned back from following the Lord. And the Lord will not be with you" (Numbers 14:41-43).

As you might imagine, they did not listen. Neither Moses, God, or the ark of the covenant accompanied them, and the Amalekites and Canaanites swooped down on this misguided band from the hill country and soundly defeated them. A reckless disobedience again plagued the Israelites. This ill-fated escapade confirmed their rebellious nature. God's previous judgment against them proved sound. The psalmist gave voice to God's feelings concerning these Israelites who were doomed to die in the wilderness.

> For forty years I loathed *that* generation,
> And said they are a people who err in their heart,
> And they do not know My ways
> (Psalms 95:11).

Deep down in their hearts, error thrived and flowed out in disobedient behaviors. Please note, this was not error in what they cognitively knew, but was instead, error within their hearts. A faith had formed in their hearts that did not correspond with

God's desires for them. Their hearts only had room for one god: themselves. From the Lord's point of view, their faith was faithless. Their ways were not His ways. What a sad legacy to leave—the generation that God "loathed." My friends, let's make sure we pay close attention to how we allow our hearts to develop. If we embrace the wrong things, our hearts will become corrupted. As we take on the attributes of Jesus in our churches, let His love flow through us, and perhaps we will be known as a church that God *adores*. Now that's a legacy. That's the Lord's church!

Parting Thoughts

A few things come to mind that I would like to leave with you. First, many of us who have conducted one-one-one Bible studies with non-Christians have probably helped bring some of them to a pivotal moment with the gospel message only to see them turn away from its promises. They believe in God. They believe Jesus is His Son and went to the cross for our sins. They believe the Bible is God's authoritative Word. They stand at the juncture of entering the "Promised Land" and becoming a child of God, yet they turn their backs on the wonderful salvation that awaits them.

If someone truly understands the grace God extends to them through Christ Jesus, why would they ever turn down so rich a gift? For many, the world offers something they are not ready to give up. Whether living in an illicit relationship, chasing wealth, or partying hard on weekends, they will not give up some part of their lifestyle or live hypocritically and accept Christ. They have weighed the outcomes and made a choice. These situations are truly heartbreaking.

Another couple of reasons for not accepting the gospel routinely come into play. Some people believe most of the Bible's truths, but they do not believe God will forgive them for a particular sin that they committed. For them, it was just too heinous for even God to forgive them. Other folks will come to a solid understanding of the gospel, but will not put on Christ because they believe their newfound beliefs will throw a condemning light on a loved one. Sometimes we need to see to our own salvation first, so we can throw a life preserver to another. That's probably what most of our loved ones would want for us as well. Nevertheless, I do not want to try to diminish the power of either of these rationales, because when you encounter them, they are strong motivators for people not to accept the gospel.

You can add to these aforementioned reasons, but nevertheless, they're enough to cause you to reflect on such dilemmas. However one might choose to proceed in such situations, do nothing that will sacrifice your relationship with these individuals. Remember, they were on the cusp of accepting Christ. Hopefully, you can continue to study with them and directly address their issues *over time*. Please note that I said *over time*. Respect where they are and continue to bring additional insights from God's Word into their lives. Recognize the power that resides in God's Word and just keep bringing its heart-changing concepts into their lives. We are trying to help develop a saving faith in an individual, and this may take time. Pray for them, and ask God what you should specifically study. Don't give up on them, even if you have to take a break from your studies together. They probably have a lot to process. Ask God to open up an additional opportunity to continue your studies in the future. God is patient with them to come to repentance, so you need to be as well. Continue to love on them, care about them, and bring the goodness of God into their lives through good deeds. Entering the "Promised Land" (Christian life) may be a little scary for them so walk beside them if they invite you. It's a wonderful and worthy walk.

Secondly, the author of Hebrews warns his audience of the danger that they could fall short of entering God's eternal rest because of an unbelieving heart (Hebrews 3:12-4:13). He uses the exodus generation's failure to enter the Promised Land as an example to demonstrate how we could also miss out on the promise to enter "God's rest." As Hebrews describes "God's rest," it appears we enter a spiritual rest at our conversion to Christ, though it comes to its full realization when Christ returns. However you choose to interpret the meaning of "God's rest," the Christian must possess faith in Christ to enter it.[61] In this passage, the Israelites who were punished to wander and die in the wilderness were characterized as sinners, disobedient, and by unbelief (3:17-19). Note how the Hebrews' writer then warns us today.

> For indeed we have had good news preached to us, just as they also; but the word they heard did not profit them, because it was not united by faith in those who heard (Hebrews 4:2).

The Hebrew nation had the good news spoken to them that God would give them the Promised Land. Caleb and Joshua encouraged the panic-stricken Israelites to overcome their fear and realize that God would protect them and deliver on His promise. Yet they just did not totally embrace the promise, and unbelief in it was their downfall. Today, the good news comes to us in the form of the gospel. This good news' destination is the human heart (spiritually, of course), where we want it to become permanently imprinted. Our cognitive understanding of the gospel serves to undergird the faith that is formed in our hearts. Always remember, our conversion should come about from a faith in what God has done in Christ Jesus. Flowing from the faith that continues to develop in our hearts will hopefully be the types of behaviors that God has outlined in His Word for His people. Paul stated that the gospel allows the Christian to become "obedient from the heart" (Romans 6:17) and walk in righteousness.

Unfortunately, the author of Hebrews kicked off this lengthy set of verses with the following warning.

> Take care, brethren, that there not be in any one of you an
> evil, unbelieving heart that falls away from the living God.
> But encourage one another day after day, as long as it is *still*
> called "Today," so that none of you will be hardened by the
> deceitfulness of sin (Hebrews 3:12-13).

Sin is deceitful. We rationalize away the truth of God for lies.
Often these falsehoods come in attractive packages. Along the
way, our faith becomes damaged and our hearts hardened. Sin is
insidious. So yes, encourage one another! Spiritually, encourage
one another! If someone is spiritually growing in her faith, praise
her accomplishments, and encourage her to continue. If she is
caught up in sin, gently address the situation with her, and
encourage her to turn away from the sin, seek forgiveness, and
stay on a godly course.

As the discussion of entering God's rest comes to a close, the
Hebrews' writer provides us some wise counsel.

> For the word of God is living and active and sharper than any
> two-edged sword, and piercing as far as the division of soul and
> spirit, of both joints and marrow, and able to judge the thoughts
> and intentions of the heart (Hebrews 4:12).

God's Word works in powerful ways on our hearts if we let
it. We need to allow it to guide our development, as we use its
power to reflect on our character and behaviors. God's Word
hones right in on our areas of brokenness that we need to address.
And remember, the Spirit wields as a sword the mighty Word of
God to prepare our hearts to withstand the schemes of Satan
(Ephesians 6:17). What a mighty duo God has given us to help
us in our transformation!

God loved the spirit of Caleb who followed Him fully, and thus
allowed him to enter the Promised Land (Numbers 14:24). May
we allow God to create in us just such a spirit, as we constantly
pray these words of the psalmist.

Search me, O God, and know my heart;
Try me and know my anxious thoughts;
And see if there be any hurtful way in me,
And lead me in the everlasting way
(Psalms 139:23-24).

Lastly, I introduced this chapter with what convinced me to step out on faith concerning a passion that I believed that God had placed on my heart. Perhaps, you as well feel such a passion to serve the Lord in some capacity. Many such passions do not require you to leave your job or move to another state or country. God may have you right where He wants you to carry out His purpose for you. Be careful how you judge your passion, and try to view it through God's perspective. To you, it may seem miniscule, but to Him, He sees eternal ramifications for others as you undertake this work of service for Him. Remember, let's do our part and plant those seeds of faith, and let Him provide the growth (1 Corinthians 3:5-7). With regard to evaluating your passion, I would like to encourage you to seek out a Christian brother or sister whom you view as spiritually insightful. Share with him or her your passion and what's going on in your life in relationship to it and seek their advice. You may want to pursue wise counsel from a couple of other trusted spiritual confidants, too. And whatever you do...pray, pray, and pray about it.

May God bless your life of faith in His Son. He loves you so much. Now on to that eternal Promised Land! And by the way, bring some friends and relatives with you.

Questions

1. Why did the Israelites not enter the Promised Land and were subjected to wander in the wilderness for 40 years?

2. How would you characterize a grumbler? What are some of the consequences that can occur from incessant grumbling in a

church? Are you prone to grumbling? If so, how should you go about stopping it?

3. In what ways were the faithless spies' report and the Israelites' panic-stricken response an affront to God? What was God's assessment of the spies and the Israelites?

4. What is church leadership's role regarding grumblers? Why is this important?

5. How do you feel about your faith developmentally? What do you need to address? How should you go about it?

6. Do you feel a passion to serve God in a given capacity? Explain not only the passion, but what makes you believe it is from God? What course of action should you take to verify it and then step out on faith?

7. Thinking back over this entire book what is the most significant thing you learned? How do you believe God wants you to use this lesson?

ENDNOTES

Chapter 1

1   Amy Shira Teitel, "How Little Vibrations Break Big Rockets: Inside the Dreaded 'Pogo Effect'," *Popular Science*, (24 September 2016) [on-line article]; available from *http://www.popsci.com/how-little-vibrations-break-big-rockets*; accessed 8 February 2017.

2   Hans Wilhelm Hertzberg, *1 & 2 Samuel*, The Old Testament Library, (Philadelphia, PA: Westminster Press, 1964), 202.

3   James E. Smith, *1 & 2 Samuel*, The College Press NIV Commentary, (Joplin, MO: College Press, 2000), 295.

4   Robert D. Bergen, *1, 2 Samuel*, The New American Commentary, vol. 7, (Nashville, TN: Broadman & Holman, 2002), 252.

5   Ibid., 245-46.

6   Ibid., 249.

7   Smith, *1 & 2 Samuel*, 300.

8   Clarence Edward Macartney, *The Way of a Man with a Maid* (Nashville, TN: Cokesbury Press, 1931), 84-85.

9   For a thorough exposition of overcoming evil with good see chapter 7 in my book; Mike O'Neal, *Created for Good Deeds* (Nashville, TN: 21st Century Christian, 2016).

Chapter 2

10 Craig S. Keener, Acts: *An Exegetical Commentary*, vol. 2, (Grand Rapids, MI: Baker Academic, 2013), 1186.

11 Ibid., 1189.

12 James Hastings, *The Greater Men and Women of the Bible* (Edinburg: T & T Clark, 1914), 63.

13 William L. Lane, *Hebrews 9-13*, Word Biblical Commentary, vol. 47b, (Dallas, TX: Word Books, 1991), 518-19.

14 Gordon D. Fee, *Paul's Letter to the Philippians*, New International Commentary, (Grand Rapids, MI: Eerdmans, 1995), 411.

Chapter 3

15 James E. Smith, *1 & 2 Samuel*, The College Press NIV Commentary, (Joplin, MO: College Press, 2000), 460.

16 Ibid., 349.

17 Robert Alter, *The David Story: A Translation with Commentary of 1 and 2 Samuel* (New York: W. W. Norton & Company, 1999), 329.

18   P. Kyle McCarter, *II Samuel*, The Anchor Bible, vol. 9, (New York: Doubleday, 1984), 373.

19   Walter Bruegemann, *First and Second Samuel*, Interpretation, (Louisville, KY: John Knox Press, 1990), 308.

20   J. P. Fokkelman, *Narrative Art and Poetry in the Books of Samuel*, vol. 1 (Netherlands: Van Gorcum, 1981), 201.

21   David Kinnaman, *UnChristian: What a New Generation Thinks about Christianity...And Why It Matters* (Grand Rapids, MI: Baker Books, 2007), 26.

Chapter 4

22   Merrill F. Unger, *The New Unger's Bible Dictionary*, ed. R. K. Harrison (Chicago: Moody Press, 1988), 154.

23   Smith, *1 & 2 Samuel*, 61.

24   Bergen, *1, 2 Samuel*, 81.

Chapter 5

25   Ibid., 221.

26   Ibid., 223.

27   Joseph Lozovyy, *Saul, Doeg, Nabal, and the "Son of Jesse:" Readings in 1 Samueluel 16-25* (New York: T&T Clark, 2009), 93.

28   Alter, *The David Story*, 138.

29   Fokkelman, *Narrative Art and Poetry in the Books of Samuel*, 391.

Chapter 6

30   Josephus, *Antiquities of the Jews*, 18.5.1.

31   Josephus, *Antiquities of the Jews*, 18.5.2.

32   D. A. Carson, *Matthew*, The Expositor's Bible Commentary, vol. 8, (Grand Rapids: Zondervan, 1984), 338.

33   William L. Lane, *The Gospel According to Mark*, The New International Commentary on the New Testament, (Grand Rapids: Eerdmans, 1974), 216.

34   Josephus, *Antiquities of the Jews*, 18.5.4.

35   Lane, *The Gospel According to Mark*, 215 & 220.

36   For a dissenting opinion as to the nature of Salome's dance see Harold W. Hoehner, *Herod Antipas* (Cambridge: University Press, 1972), 156-57.

37   Ibid., 221.

38   C. S. Mann, *Mark*, The Anchor Bible, (New York: Doubleday, 1986), 297.

39   David E. Garland, *Mark*, The NIV Application Commentary, (Grand Rapids: Zondervan, 1996), 244.

40   Larry W. Hurtado, *Mark*, New International Biblical Commentary, (Peabody, MA: Hendrickson Publishers, 1989), 98.

41   Garland, *Mark*, 244-45.

42   Ibid., 245.

43   Craig S. Keener, *Matthew*, The IVP New Testament Commentary Series, (Downers Grove, IL: InterVarsity Press, 1997), 252.

44   Carson, *Matthew*, 339.

45   Hoehner, *Herod Antipas*, 14.

46   Macartney, *The Way of a Man with a Maid*, 157.

47   Shirley Tracy, "Cleveland Native, Returns from Record Setting Space Mission," *Connection Magazine* (October 2002) [on-line magazine]; *http://connectionmagazine.org/2002_10_/ts_space_mission.htm*; Internet; accessed 5 August 2005.

48   Josephus, *Antiquities of the Jews*, 18.7.1-2.

49   Lane, *The Gospel According to Mark*, 211.

50   Clarence E. Macartney, *Chariots of Fire* (Grand Rapids: Kregel Publications, 1994), 32-33.

Chapter 7

51   Dennis Gaertner, *Acts*, The College Press NIV Commentary, (Joplin, MO: College Press, 1993), 307. (see Darrell L. Bock, *Acts*, Baker Exegetical Commentary on the New Testament, Grand Rapids: Baker Academic, 2007, 607-08.)

52   Richard N. Longenecker, "Acts," in *The Expositor's Bible Commentary*, ed. Frank E. Gaebelein (Grand Rapids: Zondervan, 1981), 9:502-03.

53   Ibid., 9:503.

54   Ibid., 9:503-04.

55   Bock, *Acts*, 612.

56   M. Robert Mulholland, *An Invitation to a Journey: A Road Map for Spiritual Formation* (Downers Grove, IL: InterVarsity Press,1993), 26.

Chapter 8

57   Thomas Jones, "Reaching the Heavens: An Astronaut's Journey," *St. Anthony Messenger* (June 2004) [magazine on-line]; available from *http://www.americancatholic.org/Messenger/Jun2004/Feature1.asp*; Internet; accessed 19 August 2000.

58   Brant Lee Doty, *Numbers*, Bible Study Textbook Series, (Joplin, MO: College Press, 1973), 144.

59   Philip J. Budd, *Numbers*, Word Biblical Commentary, vol. 5, (Waco, TX: Word Books, 1984), 147.

60   Gordon J. Wenham, *Numbers*, Tyndale Old Testament Commentaries, vol. 4, (Downers Grove, IL: InterVarsity Press, 1981), 136.

61   Neil R. Lightfoot, *Jesus Christ Today: A Commentary on the Book of Hebrews* (Grand Rapids, MI: Baker Book House, 1976), 96.